U0568208

● 乾 陵 博 物 馆

丝路胡人外来风

唐代胡俑展

Exotic Flavor of the Foreigners
on the Silk Road

Terracotta Hu Man of the Tang Dynasty

文物出版社

Exotic Flavor of the Foreigners on the Silk Road

Terracotta Hu Man of the Tang Dynasty

Consultants: **Sun Ji Yang Hong**

Planner: **Ge Chengyong**

Director of the Editorial Committee: **Zhao Rong**

Vice Directors of the Editorial Committee: **Guo Xianzeng Liu Yunhui**

Editor-in-Chief: **Fan Yingfeng**

Associate Editors: **Ma Li Zhang Jianlin Liang Zi**

Editorial Committee: **E Jun Cheng Jianzheng Jia Qiang Ma Wenting Wang Xiu Kong Zhengyi Fan Yanping Ren Zhoufang Xi Liguang Yang Yunshan Yang Jianguo Chen Yande Wang Pingyi Liu Xiangyang**

Writing & Data Preparation: **Jia Jianwei Han Jianwu Zhang Zhipan Liu Daiyun Xiao Qi Wang Quanjun Ge Hong He Zhengquan Duan Guoqiang Jing Hongwei Wang Wujun Ding Yongzhen Li Langtao Hou Xiaobin Song Shaoyu**

Photographers: **Wang Baoping Zhao Guangtian**

Format-Designers: **Zhang Xin**

Translators: **Fang Jun Wang Yuanyuan**

丝路胡人外来风——唐代胡俑展

学 术 顾 问

孙 机 杨 泓

策 划

葛承雍

编委会主任

赵 荣

编委会副主任

郭宪曾 刘云辉

主 编

樊英峰

副 主 编

马 力 张建林 梁 子

编 委

俄 军 成建正 贾 强 马文廷
王 绣 孔正一 樊延平 任周方
习黎光 杨云善 杨建国 陈彦德
王平义 刘向阳

撰稿及资料

贾建威 韩建武 张志攀 刘呆运
肖 琦 王全军 葛 洪 贺正权
段国强 景宏伟 王武君 丁永振
李浪涛 侯晓斌 宋少宇

摄 影

王保平 赵广田

编 排

张 鑫

英 文 翻 译

方 骏 王媛媛

Contents

目 录

序 言

◎ 孙 机 (中国国家博物馆研究员)

　　胡俑是古俑中特殊的一群，只见于隋唐时期，宋代已不再出现，北朝墓出土的"胡俑"，其实大多数代表鲜卑人；鲜卑墓主随葬鲜卑俑，固属事理之常，与唐人以胡俑随葬有别。再往前在汉画像石里，却可以看到大规模胡汉交战的场面，时代的特点又自不同。

　　唐俑中之"胡"，大抵指粟特人。能区别出来的还有昆仑人，但较少见。至于区别更少见的大食人和其他民族，目前仍难准确做到，兹不讨论。粟特人是居住在中亚河中地区即泽拉夫善河流域的半农半商民族。当时的大商队都以武力自保，所以粟特人也尚武。然而与十六国时期以武装入侵的方式进入中原的北方各族不同，叩关的粟特人多以通商的面貌出现。尽管贞观年间康国大首领康艳典充任蒲昌海（今罗布泊）石城镇之镇使时（《新唐书·地理志》），"胡人随之，因成聚落"。其后，在石城镇外又筑起胡人聚居的新城、蒲桃城和萨毗城（s.367号《沙州伊州地志》），仿佛是一些殖民的据点；但唐政府以宽容的态度处之。这时入华的粟特人大都生活在此类聚落中。起初，他们几乎与唐代社会格格不入。粟特人信仰火祆教，然而并不外传，不曾有过译成汉文的祆教经典，各地之祆祠唐政府也"禁民祈祭"（《新唐书·百官志》）；在宗教上与信仰佛、道的唐人完全隔绝。在婚姻上，粟特人实行血亲通婚。《隋书·西域传》说粟特人"妻其姊妹，及母子相禽兽"。唐·慧超《往五天竺国传》说粟特人"极恶风俗，婚姻交杂，纳母及姊妹为妻"。唐·杜环《经行记》也说："寻寻（指祆教徒）蒸报于诸夷狄中最甚。"西安出土的《唐苏谅妻马氏墓志》中，就记下了祆教徒近亲通婚的事例（《考古》1964年第9期）。这种风俗，自唐人看来，实属悖逆伦常，为情理所不容。在丧葬制度上，祆教经典《阿维斯陀经》规定，要将死者置于山间，让狗嗜鸟啄。但萨珊波斯实行天葬，尸体虽任鸟啄，却不令野兽吞食。粟特人则又不然。唐·韦节《西蕃记》说，康国于城外，"别筑一院，院内养狗。每有人死，即往取尸，置此院内，令狗食人肉尽，收骸骨埋殡"。《旧唐书·李晟传》所记太原"黄坑"，也是狗食死人之处，似亦为流寓当地的粟特人治丧之所。为哀悼死者，其亲属或劖面截耳。这些做法，并令唐人不胜惊诧骇怪。当然，如果他们在本乡行施自己的风俗，外人可不必置喙。但大批粟特人却留恋唐之富庶，乐不思归，不愿"还蕃"；这样就产生了一个如何找到在这里长期生活下去的出路、实际上也就是如何进入唐代社会的问题。

　　当唐王朝的统治得到巩固后，大部分聚落被编为乡里，入籍的粟特人之从事农业者依均田法受田，并承担相应的赋税兵役。他们与汉族农民杂居，且互相通婚，较易汉化。那些继续经商的：未入籍者称"客胡"；入籍者则成为"当县夷胡户"，其籍贯"属西、庭、伊等州府者，验有公文，原于本贯以东来往"（s.1344号《开元户部格断简》）。也就是说入籍的胡商只能在其户籍所在的边州以东的内地进行贸易。而"客胡"虽然也不允许捆载内地产品任意"入蕃"，但可以从域外运货进来，比入籍者方便。所以这两部分粟特商人遂互相配合，操控丝路上的贸易。长安西市中胡商尤多，"西市胡（商）"成为当时的一个专门名称。经他们转贩而来的西方物品常为论者推重，誉之为"撒马尔罕金桃"。虽然由此带来了若干西方器物的造型与纹饰，丰富了唐代的工艺制作。但其中大部分为奢侈品，或用途不广的奇货；远不能和16世纪传来的美洲作物、19世纪传来的欧洲机械相比，于发展社会生产、改善民众生活的作用至尠。而且未入籍的客胡流动性大，虽他们善于适应，但很难被看成是社会中之稳定的因素。

不过入唐既久，且已脱离聚落约束的粟特人，逐渐不循旧制。改奉摩尼教、景教以及佛教的不在少数；唐代的佛教大师释法藏（见《宋高僧传》）、释伽跋摩（见《大唐西域求法高僧传》）等都是粟特人。其精英分子更努力接受汉文化，供职唐廷的大有人在。他们不但担任译语、将作、监牧等方面的职务，还有成进士、做文官的。然而这些人，包括未解体以前的粟特聚落成员，都不会出现在胡俑中。只有贫困的粟特移民，居留的时间已长，对唐土风情知之已稔，已基本华化者，才能为汉族大户所收容；甚至也只有其中的"家生子"，才能受到充分信任。因为随葬的胡俑代表的是这类人，而不是人地两生的初来者，更不会是精英阶层；所以考察在现实生活中沦为厮役奴婢的胡俑，只能为唐代社会中的粟特人这幅大画卷揭开一角，其中还不可避免地被涂上一层墓主人所属意的色彩。由于粟特人"十岁骑羊逐沙鼠"（李益诗，《全唐诗》卷二八二），懂得畜牧，所以牵驼驭马的胡俑相当多。可是无论俑或驼、马，以及所驮之物，无疑悉数代表墓主人的财产。研究者不宜离开这一基本事实而过度引申。比如有人把它们看成是丝路上的商队的一部分；甚至驼囊上的兽面装饰也被认为即《酉阳杂俎》所称"刻氎为形，盛于皮袋"的祆神（《唐研究》第7卷）。而如本书页40所收陕西乾县唐章怀太子墓出土的三彩骆驼，造型诚如其说；但章怀太子既不经商又不信祆教，与丝路贸易及祆神均不相干。又辽宁省博物馆所藏朝阳唐代鲁善都墓出土之彩绘骑驼俑，骑者既是汉人面相，朝阳又僻在北方，也说明此驼与丝路上的商队没有直接关系。而陕西户县元代贺氏墓出土的驮马，其驮囊上亦饰兽面。元代不流行祆教，此驮囊更与祆神无涉。

粟特人长于音乐歌舞，唐代的胡人乐俑颇不罕见，西安鲜于庭诲墓出土的骆驼载乐俑尤为著名。本书页186所收西安西郊枣园唐俾失十囊墓出土的乐俑共6人，所奏乐器有二弦琵琶（疑即勿雷）、答腊鼓、横笛、竖笛等，另有引吭作歌者，其安排与上述载乐俑差近。俾失十囊为突厥首领。《册府元龟》卷九七四载，开元四年四月"突厥俾失州大首领伊罗友阙颉斤十囊来降，封其妻阿失那氏为雁门郡夫人，以向化宠之也"。此人卒于开元十二年，居唐仅8年，随葬之乐俑胡貌唐装，疑非其本族，此时粟特之附突厥者人数甚众，所以这些乐俑可能也是粟特人。不过令人奇怪的是，胡俑及相关之美术作品中出现的舞者皆为舞胡腾的胡人男子，而舞胡旋、柘枝之胡人女子则不经见。其实胡人女子中之酒家胡姬，在唐代风头正健。李白诗"胡姬貌如花，当炉笑春风"；"胡姬招素手，延客醉金樽"（《李太白集》卷三，卷一八）；均反映出偕胡姬置酒饮谑之状。但红粉浮浪，诗句轻薄；再考虑到其祆教之"恶俗"的背景，则胡姬在当时人眼中一般不被视作良家妇女。元曲中涉及男女私情时仍常常扯上祆教，如《货郎旦》第三折："祆庙火，宿世缘，牵牛织女长生愿。"甚至明清时妓院中供奉的行业神白眉神，据刘铭恕先生考证，亦由祆神转化而来（《边疆研究论丛》1942—1944年卷）。因此在唐代上层人士用于葬礼的陶俑中没有她们的位置，出土物中迄今尚未发现可以被确认的女胡俑。唐代男胡俑的面目剽悍，有的且接近狰狞，胡女的面型大约也不尽符合唐人的审美习惯。这时如对人说"子貌类胡"，绝不是一句恭维的话。"如花"云云，不过是吟咏时即兴遣辞而已。更由于在社会心理上把她们定格为风尘冶艳之尤，遂使之难以在正式场合抛头露面。有鉴于此，唐代之带粟特血统的贵妇，常特地攀附汉族烈女贞妇的节操，用以标榜。如洛阳出土的仪凤二年《曹氏墓志》，其父名毗沙，显然是胡人。但志文中说她"贞顺闲雅，令范端详"；"四德周备，六行齐驱"；"孝同梁妇，节比义姑"（《千唐志斋藏志》）。这些诔墓之词可能不尽是实录。因为同出于洛阳的《安师墓志》（龙朔三年）与《康达墓志》（总章二年），文字竟几乎全同（均见《隋唐五代墓志汇编·洛阳卷》）。炮制者依样葫芦，照猫画虎，其中的假大空，自不待言。

真正广泛吸纳粟特移民从事的职业是当雇佣兵。《大唐西域记》说康国"兵马强盛，多诸赭羯。赭羯之人，其性勇烈，视死如归，战无前敌"。赭羯亦作柘羯，意为勇士。本书页192之胡人骑俑，裸露上身，肌肉饱绽，或即代表侍卫永泰公主的一名柘羯。唐的建立颇赖突厥兵之助，所以自始就有任用蕃将的传统。特别是到了玄宗朝，由于均田之制已弛，建立在均田制上的府兵确已"不堪攻战"，蕃将统领的军队已成为国家主要的武装力量。虽说其中包括蕃汉兵卒，而且蕃人亦不尽是粟特，但九姓胡毕竟占有相当大的比例。高适诗中甚至说："控弦尽用阴山儿，登阵常骑大宛马"（《全唐诗》卷二一三），可以想见当时唐军中胡骑之众。蕃将为了取得信任，每每竭力作输诚效忠的表白："忠勤奉主，操等松筠；委质称臣，心贞昆玉"（《康元敬墓志》，见《隋唐五代墓志汇编·洛阳卷》）。但实际上像安金藏、石演芬等之能做到忠于一姓者，亦不多见（《新唐书》安、石本传）。其民风或如《西域记》所说："风俗浇讹，多行诡诈。"《旧唐书·突厥传》也说："胡人贪冒，性多翻覆。"以安禄山为例，他在唐玄宗面前的表演，如《安禄山事迹》所记，可谓矫情作态，已臻极致。安禄山"腹缓及膝"，当被问起其中何物时，他就说："唯赤心耳！"最后此人成为范阳、平卢、河东三镇节度使，身兼三个大军区的司令，兵刑钱谷，生杀予夺，尽操一人之手；其麾下的镇兵人数相当于全国兵额的36％。他的反叛，成为李唐由盛而衰的分界线。致令杜甫悲哀地感叹："羯胡事主终无赖，词客哀时且未还"（《全唐诗》卷二三〇）。这场叛乱不仅给国家造成了无可弥补的伤害，也使杜甫饱受颠沛流离之苦。安史叛军中就有不少柘羯。围睢阳城时，"有大酋被甲，引柘羯千骑，麾帜乘城招巡"（《新唐书·张巡传》）。这些柘羯骑兵虽早已湮灭在时间的长河中，但从本图集页138页之骑具装马、戴虎头磕脑的胡俑身上，却仿佛仍能看到那个令人震怖的历史时刻中之粟特铁骑的影子。

Foreword

◎ By Sun Ji

Terracotta foreigner is a special case of the ancient terracotta figurines, which only appeared in the Sui and Tang Dynasties. The figurines unearthed from the tombs of the Northern Dynasties were modeled after the people of Xianbei. Using such terracotta figurines as funerary objects was natural to the tomb owners who were also from the Xianbei tribe, while the terracotta foreigners buried in Chinese tombs of Tang was another story. As to the stone relieves of the Han Dynasty that recorded the wars between the people of Han and Barbarians, we can notice more marked differences.

The terracotta foreigners of Tang were mostly modeled after the Sogdians, with the exception of a few Kunlun slaves. As for the people from Arab and other nations, it is something beyond discussion for the difficulties in identifying them. The Sogdians of Central Asia lived on farming and trade, and a martial spirit was also necessary for the self-defense of their caravans. They entered into China as merchants instead of the invaders. Although a Sogdian colony was established in the area of present Lop Nur during the era of Zhenguan, the Tang government was tolerant towards them. The Sogdians in China were mainly organized in such colony, being out of tune with the society of Tang. Zoroastrianism only spread within their communities. There was no Chinese version of Zoroastrian manuscripts, and the people of Han were prohibited to worship it. According to the official historical documents, travel books and the epitaph, consanguineous marriage was popular in Sogdiana, which was against the Chinese ethical tradition. Moreover, the Zoroastrian burial ritual noted that the body of the dead should be placed in mountain, with remains being taken away by dog or bird. The so-called Huang Keng of Taiyuan was said to be a spot for such Sogdian ritual. More unacceptable to Chinese people was the self-mutilation for expressing the deep mourning to the dead. The Sogdians were unwilling to go homeland because of the prosperity of Tang China, so they had to find an access to integrate into the Chinese society.

The Sogdian colonies were included into the administration system after a stable regime of Tang was finally formed. The Sogdians listed in the household register could get some land, and were requested to pay taxes and serve in the military accordingly. They also began to marry the people of Han. The unregistered Sogdian merchants were prohibited to transport goods from China to foreign countries at random, but it was more convenient for them to import goods into China than those registered ones who could trade in the regions east to the prefectures they resided. The former, therefore, together with the latter cooperated in controlling the trade on the Silk Road. Sogdian merchants crowded the western market of Chang'an, and were famed for their exotic products marked as "the golden peach of Samarkant". The style and decoration patterns of these products influenced the art of Tang. But most of them were luxury items with limited market potential that didn't help a lot on the social development and living condition of China. In addition, the high mobility of unregistered Sogdian merchants was regarded as an unstable factor to the political power.

The Sogdians in Tang China, however, didn't follow their own traditions generally and converted to Manichaeism, Nestorianism or Buddhism. Some of them even became Buddhist masters or high-ranking officials of the central government, but they were not modeled as the terracotta foreigners. On the contrary, those deeply sinicized ones in poverty who could be accepted by the rich families of Han were the prototypes of the terracotta foreigners. To the comprehensive research on the Sogdians of Tang, the study of the terracotta foreign slaves is just a tip of iceberg. Scholars should bear in mind that the Sogdians are mainly modeled as figurines leading camel or horse for being good at livestock raising, while the commodities on the back of camel or horse simply stand for the possession of the tomb owners. It is inconsiderate to suppose that such terracotta foreigners reflect the caravans traveled on the Silk Road, and the bag adorned with a demon's mask on the back of camel is an icon of Zoroastrian deity. Similar bags can be observed on a tri-colored glazed pottery from the tomb of Prince Zhanghuai (see page 9 of the present book), a pottery camel housed in Liaoning Museum and another pottery horse unearthed from a tomb of the Yuan Dynasty in Shanxi, which indicates that such bag has nothing to do with trade on the Silk Road or Zoroastrian deity.

The Sogdians were good at music and dancing, so the pottery figurines of musicians were not rare. On page 169 of this book, we can see six pottery musicians playing Pipa or flute discovered from a tomb of Tang in Xi'an. According to the related historical materials, the tomb owner was a clan leader from Turk who had lived in Tang China for 8 years and died in the 12th year of Kaiyuan era. From the appearance, we doubt the pottery musicians were actually modeled after the Sogdians. More interesting is that all the pottery dancers are male foreigners. In fact, female foreigners were active as waitresses of the wine-booths at that time, but they were embodiments of debauchery in the eyes of Chinese people because of the Zoroastrian background. Zoroastrianism even became a scapegoat in the dramas regarding adultery of the Yuan Dynasty, and it is suggested that the trade God worshipped in the brothels of the Ming and Qing Dynasties was originated from Zoroastrianism. Hence no pottery female Sogdians can be found in the tombs of those Chinese with high social positions. The facial features of the terracotta foreigners are extraordinary from the beauty appreciation of Tang, especially the female Sogdians' seductive charms shut them out of the formal occasions. Noblewomen with Sogdian origin in Tang China, then, indulged in a pursuit of virtue and pureness of Chinese women. From the epitaphs of the Sogdian women from Luoyang, we can conclude a formula full of empty words extolling the virtue of them.

The Sogdians of vigorous, fearless and gallant characters was mostly employed into the Tang army. The terracotta horse-rider from the tomb of Princess Yongtai (refer to page 170) might be a guard of the princess. Turkish army contributed a lot to the foundation of Tang, thus initiated a military tradition of employing foreign generals in Tang China. During the reign of Emperor Xuanzong, the Equal-field System and the Mansion Army System didn't work, so the foreign generals, a great majority of whom were Sogdians, played an important role in Tang army. It seems that they endeavored to show loyalty for gaining the emperors' confidence from the context of their epitaphs, but few of them devoted wholeheartedly. For instance, An Lushan, a greedy and capricious Sogdian, tried his best to get the favor of Xuanzong and gained astonishing military power in North-east China. But his cataclysmic rebellion, as a turning point in the Tang Dynasty's fortunes, effectively ended the strong rule by the central government. An's rebel force consisted of many sogdians who already became a part of our remembrance. The terracotta foreigner on page 138 of the present book, however, reminds us of the Sogdian horse-riders at that soul-stirring period.

前　言

◎ 杨　泓（中国社科院考古研究所研究员、博士生导师）

　　李唐王期，是中国古代历史上一个颇为开放的时期，承袭着北朝的文化传统。
而在十六国南北朝时期，曾长期生长于北部或西北边疆的古代少数民族，纷纷迁入中
原，并建立政权，取代汉族成为统治民族，促成各民族文化的大融合。但是在原居中
原的汉人看来，那些民族如匈奴、鲜卑等就是胡人或东胡。而这些民族建立政权以
后，特别是如拓跋鲜卑统一北方与南朝对峙以后，则又将在其西北的西域人士称为
"胡"。不过当时社会中并不排斥胡人，而且还设有管理在华胡人或胡人宗教的官
员，还由来华胡人充任，近年在西安陆续发现的北周安伽、史君诸墓可以为证。

　　李唐建国前，李渊、李世民父子治军，组建骑兵系仿效突厥，战马亦多取自突厥。
李唐建国之初平定群雄的征战中，军中亦有突厥将领，如西突厥特勤大奈（后赐姓史
氏），因屡有战功，累迁右武卫大将军、检校丰州都督，封窦国公。卒赠辅国大将军，
已是正第二品。此后有唐一代，武将中一直不乏"胡人"，突厥、突骑施以及昭武九姓
诸国人氏都有，还有东北的靺鞨、百济、高丽等，皆能以军功升迁高位。足见李唐王朝
时确实颇为开放，并不在乎将领的民族成分，而能因材录用。总体看来，唐代入居中土
的胡人，其身份大体可以分为上中下三层：

　　胡人中身分最高的上层人士，如前引史大奈已官居正第二品。许多胡人身为高官或
与公主皇亲等结婚，死后还有陪葬皇陵的荣誉。仅举经过考古发掘的昭陵陪葬墓为例，
其中就有突厥人阿史那忠、安国人安元寿等，他们的墓葬都具有多天井的长斜坡墓道，
精美的壁画，并有数量众多的随葬俑群。据墓志阿史那忠为右骁卫大将军，安元寿为
右威卫将军，皆为正第三品。可惜墓内随葬陶俑群均遭盗扰，所以不知其中是否有"胡
俑"。但同为昭陵陪葬墓的郑仁泰墓，死者亦官居右武卫大将军，与阿史那忠、安元寿
同属正三品，墓内随葬陶俑群保存较好，其中即有"胡俑"及着翻领胡装的俑，因此推
测阿史那、安两墓中俑群内容也应与郑墓相同，恐亦不乏"胡俑"。

　　中层的胡人，虽身无官位，多是入唐的商贾平民，但是其中许多是富有资财者，所
以唐人传奇中多有胡人与宝物的故事。另一些人则是经营酒肆商铺的商贾。此外，也有
些人入华后担任小官吏，如在西安曾发现汉文与中古波斯文合璧的苏谅妻马氏墓志，马
氏的丈夫苏谅，就是波斯萨珊朝被阿拉伯人灭亡后，流寓华土的波斯人的后裔，后被编
入神策军中。

　　下层的胡人，则是生活在社会底层的奴婢等，许多是畜养牲畜的奴仆，诗人岑参
《卫节度赤骠马歌》所咏："紫髯胡雏金剪刀，平明剪出三鬃高。"即为养马的胡人。

想当年唐廷大量购入突厥良马，自多随马群入华的养马者。胡人酒肆商铺中，亦多有服役的胡姬、胡侍。还有从事百戏杂技表演的艺人。这些胡人，生活在社会的底层，受人役使，目前出现在唐墓随葬俑群中的"胡俑"，恐怕皆以下层胡人为模写对象。

综上所述，可以看出目前我们从唐墓考古发掘中获得的"胡俑"，并不足以反映当时在唐朝版图内生活的所有入华"胡人"，而只是可以反映出入华胡人的下层，他们受当时社会居于统治地位的华胡上层人士所驱使奴役，从事养马牵驼，或供随从役使。同时，在观察研究"胡俑"时，还应注意古人制作这些陶俑的目的，本是为了随葬之用，虽然其形貌所模写的模特儿应是社会生活中的下层胡人，但是限于墓仪制度的要求，它们不是写真的艺术创作，而且所依据的"粉本"又常拘于程式化或滞后性，制作的匠师也时有部分局部改变，因此在分析这些俑像时，切忌简单地将其直接等同于社会现实事物。同时仅仅靠某些俑像似模写了"高鼻深目"或有连鬓胡须即定位为"胡人"，有时也失之简单，因为即使是观察活人，也常有失误。从中国历史上也可寻到生动的实例，如东晋十六国时期，冉闵消灭后赵政权时，大杀氐羌诸胡，看到高鼻多须者就杀。《晋书·石季龙载记》："一日之中，斩首数万。……于时高鼻多须至有滥死者半。"我们今日辨别"胡俑"时，也应以为鉴。因此仅据形貌而去推测陶俑所模拟的人像的种族或民族，是十分困难的事。

虽然从随葬陶俑群中辨识"胡俑"，有极大的局限和许多困难，但是这些俑像毕竟是今人窥知唐代下层胡人的一扇可资利用的窗口，也可以通过他们进一步了解唐代社会生活。同时唐代"胡俑"的制作常常相当精致，造型也颇生动，还可被视为艺术造诣颇高的唐代人像雕塑品，值得重视。

乾陵博物馆能够将西安地区发掘出土的唐代"胡俑"集中展示，必定能将有关唐代"胡人"的学术研讨推向新的高潮，这是令人高兴的。期望通过这次的展览和学术研讨，能推动有关唐代"胡人"的研究，取得新的更大的成就。

Introduction

◎ By Yang Hong

During the period of the Sixteen Kingdoms and the Northern and Southern Dynasties, ancient nationalities originally scattered in the North or along the North-west frontier poured into China Proper. They brought this region under the political control successively, and then caused a cultural integration. Additionally, the Tang Dynasty inherited the cultural tradition of the Northern Dynasties. All of these made the Tang Empire an era of opening-up in the ancient history of China. In the eyes of the people of Han, however, the nomadic tribes such as Huns or Xianbei, were just Barbarians (Hu) or Donghu. After establishing powers in North China, the nomadic tribes especially Tuoba Xianbei called the residents in the West Region Hu. In fact, no prejudice against these foreigners at that time, and the central government appointed certain foreigners to be in charge of the special group in China and its religious affairs. As to this, the tombs of An Jia and Shi Jun of the Northern Dynasties unearthed in Xi'an presented strong cases.

Before the establishment of the Tang Empire, Li Yuan and his sons followed the military system of Turkish horse soldiers. Many Turkish generals served in the army to pacify separatist forces after the foundation of Tang, such as Danai (lately bestowed a family name as Shi) from Western Turk, who got promotion for his meritorious military service and was finally ranked as the second-grade official after his death. Immigrants, including people from Turk, Turgis, Sogdiana and even the tribes of Mohe, Baiji and Gaoli in the North East, always played an important role in the Tang army. They got promotion corresponding to their military exploits, which reflected an attitude of the Tang Dynasty showing great concern for appointment of people of talent without respect to their backgrounds. According to the social status, the immigrants in Tang China could be generally divided into three groups:

Firstly, foreigners in higher positions. They were nobilities by birth, or maintained marriage relationship with the royal family, enjoying the honor of being buried along with the emperors. For example, the joint tombs of Zhao Mausoleum in which buried some foreigners such as Ashina Zhong from Turk and An Yuanshou from the Kingdom of An. They all had long sloping tomb passages with many skylights, exquisite wall-paintings and considerable quantities of terracotta figurines. We learn from the epitaphs that Ashina and An were generals with the third official rank. Unfortunately, it remains unknown whether any terracotta foreigners were included in the tombs for their looted condition. Nevertheless, in the well-preserved tomb of Zheng Rentai, which was also a joint one of Zhao mausoleum, we found the terracotta foreigners. Zheng had the same rank as Ashina Zhong and An Yuanshou, therefore, it is reasonable to think the last two also had terracotta foreigners as the funerary objects.

Secondly, foreign merchants of the middle class who had large fortunes instead of official positions. They inspired a popular topic of jewels and themselves documented in the literary tales of Tang. Some of them lived as wine-sellers, while others worked as low-ranking officials in the government, such as a Persian named Su Liang who escaped to China after the destroy of Sassanian Empire by Arabs and got a post in the Shence Guards according to the Chinese-Middle Persian bilingual epitaph of Lady Ma, Su's wife.

Foreigners of the underclass in Tang China were slaves, and most of them engaged in livestock raising, such as horse-feeding narrated in a poem by Cen Can, a famous poet. Because the Tang Dynasty ever imported Turkish horses in great amount, the slaves as horse-herders entered into China simultaneously. Some of the slaves served in wine-booths or shops ran by foreigners, and some of them were tumblers. Being in the lower class, they were held in bondage. The terracotta figurines found in the tombs are presumably modeled on them.

In a word, our present collection of the terracotta foreigners unearthed from the Tang tombs reflects the humble group of the underclass rather than the whole colony of the foreigners. The former was enslaved by the ruling class consisted of both Chinese and foreigners, living as cattle herder or attendant. We should bear in mind that the terracotta foreigners were funerary objects, and although they were model-based artworks, they couldn't be the realistic expression in order to fit the funeral rituals. The terracotta makers had to do some changes because of the formulation and time-lag of the prototype, therefore, we shouldn't consider the terracotta figurines completely as a mirror of the real social condition. In addition, it is not convincing to identify a terracotta figurine as a foreigner according to his Roman nose, deep-set eyes or sideburns, because this criterion is unreliable even the observation object is a living man. During the period of the Eastern Jin and the Sixteen Kingdoms, for instance, Ran Min overthrew the rule of the Later Zhao and slaughtered the people whoever had high nose bridge and beard. In light of this historical record, we should be cautious in the identification. It is doubtful to decide the race of the prototype simply by the facial feature of the terracotta figurines.

Despite the great difficulties in identifying terracotta foreigners among the collection of the terracotta figurines, the former is an important case available to us for exploring the immigrants of lower class and the social life of the Tang Dynasty. Meanwhile, the skillful and vivid terracotta foreigners attract people as statues with superb artistic attainment of Tang.

It is delighted that the Museum of Qianling Mausoleum collects and exhibits the terracotta foreigners unearthed in Xi'an, which will undoubtedly bring the study of foreigners in Tang China to another climax. Through this exhibition and academic conference, we hope a greater accomplishment can be achieved in this field.

丝路古道与唐代胡俑

◎ 葛承雍（文物出版社总编辑、教授、博士生导师）

　　乾陵博物馆举办的《丝路胡俑外来风》展览，无疑在海内外是第一次集中专题式的人物造型展览，而且这类人物主角是唐诗中描写的"琉璃宝眼紫髯须""皮肤如玉鼻如锥"那些高鼻深目、卷发长须的胡人。展览一个鲜明主题就是丝绸之路与外来民族的交流影响，通过胡俑外化形态揭示异域文明的传入，通过造型艺术直观地解读胡人入华的史料，通过历史遗产的回顾思考对未来社会更加开放的憧憬。

　　随着近年全国各地北朝和隋、唐墓发掘中胡俑不断出土，每每引起人们关注与社会反响，胡俑的形象已经深入人心、耳熟能详，虽不是俯拾皆是、蔚为大观，但也是层出不穷，过目不忘。可惜的是，没有一个博物馆愿意抓住机遇主动承办胡人专题展。而乾陵博物馆借申报丝绸之路为世界遗产之春风，举办了这样一个颇有中外交流意义的文物展览，尽管展览的胡俑是以乾陵出土收藏为主，借调了西安周边地区一些文博单位的文物，但是100多件胡人俑集中一起，汇聚一堂，图像整合的典型性已经足够了，展览规模和艺术风格也凸显了，确实令人耳目一新，赞叹不已。

　　众所周知，乾陵是初唐走向盛唐时期的皇家陵寝文化代表，已发掘的陪葬墓群中有160多件文物与丝绸之路息息相关，不仅有《客使图》、《狩猎出行图》、《打马球图》等国宝级罕见壁画，还有列入一级文物的彩绘陶俑、三彩俑70余件，其中胡人俑就有30多件。重要的是，流釉晕染、分外艳丽的三彩俑这时出现在地下世界，例如章怀太子

客使图　唐　1972年陕西省乾县
章怀太子墓出土

墓就有6件三彩胡人牵马俑，永泰公主墓出土的一批三彩胡人俑特征非常令人诧异吃惊，懿德太子墓中的胡人骑马狩猎俑也是独具特色，最高的唐三彩文武官俑和大体量骆驼俑都接近1米之高，给人的视觉冲击确实是摄人魂魄，撼人心灵，不仅雕塑彰显了史诗般的经典力作，而且喷薄出盛唐时代海纳百川的光彩。

一

　　千年前的雕塑工匠们在胡俑身上倾注自己的创作力量，赋予陶土材料以生动的灵魂，赋予静态的造型以传神的外来面貌，这不仅是艺术表现力的展现，更是当时历史生活的折射展现。《旧唐书·西戎传》记载胡人"多嗜酒，好歌舞于道路。生子必以石蜜纳口中，明胶置掌内，欲其成长口常甘言，掌持钱如胶之黏物。俗习胡书。善商贾，争分铢之利。男子年二十，即远之旁国，来适中夏，利之所在，无所不到"。胡人从中亚绿洲的一个个据点，扩散到西域周边，又经过河西走廊通道，来往于汉地中原各个城镇，除了唐代两京长安和洛阳人数众多外，流动足迹北方远涉山西、河北、北京和辽宁朝阳，南方在长沙、武昌、桂林、广州、成都等地屡屡出现，这是一条无限延长的商贸之路。其实近年研究表明，胡人职业是丰富多彩的，身份亦是多元的，不仅仅是从事贩运的胡客商贾，既有从事畜牧的牵驼养马者，也有耕田扶犁的务农者，既有酿酒酤卖的酒家胡，也有变幻百戏的卖艺者，既有侍候主人的家奴，还有进入中原后为朝廷效力的文臣武将。

　　至于胡汉血缘融合的通婚嫁娶更是普遍，侨民后裔或者二代、三代的"土生胡"，使那种在东方人看来象西方人，在西方人看来又像东方人的中亚人种，逐渐地形成了新的胡容胡貌。比较难以辨别的是，胡人作为中亚地区最古老的印欧人种，他们当时与蒙古人种的突厥人持续地进行着强迫或自愿相结合的婚姻，形成了一个民族大熔炉，仅从容貌上很难普遍认同，判定一个民族的族源更是纠缠不清。这个令人费解的人类学之谜使现代学者枉费了许多功夫，有人声称这个俑是粟特人，那个俑是波斯人；也有人推测这个俑是突厥人，那个俑是回纥人；结果只能是一本令人生疑的糊涂帐。胡人俑无疑为我们找到了认识西域以及其他民族的一面镜子，但是汉人眼中的"胡"与胡人眼中的"汉"有时真假难辨，界限模糊，鼻高须多的"类胡"者还常常遭到戏谑嘲讽，依靠胡人俑去鉴别古代国家种族很可能带来极大的误会。

　　值得注意的是，胡人俑也分不同等级，有的胡俑身为蕃将文臣属于特殊阶层，但大多数属于卫士随从；有的则身为奴婢马夫明显属于下层社会，但他们表情温雅驯服却衣着华丽；还有许多歌舞音乐的杂耍表演伎形象则属于另类等级，取悦主人扮演着仆人的角色；身份等级与神态禀性是绝对不同的。但大多数胡俑是以社会下层面貌出现的，他们摆放在墓葬里就是在阴间继续侍奉故去的主人，如果说他们是一类"弱势人群"恐不为过，尽管千年之后我们已无法详解这些胡俑的内心感情、追求愿望和生活处境，但从墓中掺杂摆放的位置可以感受到他们的困顿无奈与底层命运。

　　胡人俑作为一种视觉文化的作品，既不像陵墓外大体量的石刻雕像那样巍然屹立，又不像棺椁内晶莹状的玉石雕刻那样小巧玲珑，而是在墓葬中壁龛或者墓室里摆放的真人替代品，表现的是"人"的"面"和"体"，每一个俑都从属于为死者建立的特殊象征空间里，他的形象是"活的"。尽管每个胡人俑似乎表现的单独个体，实际上胡人俑都融入群体之中，有些甚至成为"程式化"的表现。在那些违礼越制、推崇厚葬的墓室里，成百上千的陶俑作为送葬明器陈列于墓所，"偶人象马，雕饰如生"；"炫耀路人，破产倾资"。还有人要赢得"孝"名以利于今后入仕做官，也大量到冥器铺去订做随葬俑。从北朝到隋唐，一般小型墓葬中就有100多个俑，河北磁县北齐湾漳墓中多达1800多个俑。仅从乾陵陪葬墓来看，永泰公主墓出土陶俑878个，懿德太子墓

各国王子举哀图 中唐 敦煌莫高窟第一五八窟

出土陶俑1065个，章怀太子墓出土700多个，这些陶俑不仅数量多，而且尺寸高，显示了皇家成员地位显赫，制作也最为精美。只不过每个墓葬中的胡人形象数量较少。

　　饶有兴味的是，所有的俑都把写实和想象结合成凝固的视觉形式，有着题材组合的变化，从而形成几组俑所构成的一个大场面。尤其是这些俑被缩小比例便于呈现集体面貌，既有规模可观的乐舞队伍，又有一群杂技表演团体，既有分立几列的显达文武勋官，又有持盾抚剑的仪仗军阵，既有女仆杂役和马夫驼手，又有架鹰携犬的出猎马队，每个场面队伍中总是夹杂着各种胡人角色，比如吹奏乐师、牵马驭手、骑驼商客、持笏臣僚、仪仗武士、狩猎骑兵等等，我们可以想象着墓主人的灵魂睡卧在石榻上，低视着众多臣下恭顺俯首者有胡人，欣赏着乐舞演出服侍宾客还有胡人，观看着狩猎活动收获而归时也有骑马载物的胡人，可以说，胡人无处不在处处在，这和当时唐境内有不少胡人聚居之处相匹配。胡人生活面既广且深，他们的形象被塑造成各色陶

俑，既象征着各族归顺、各国臣服的心态，又显摆着墓主人"超规格"的世间生活，彷佛在地下世界可以无限延续以至奢华永恒。

二

　　唐代石刻雕塑我们见过不少，但在墓葬中的却很少，大概石刻费时费工费钱，不如泥塑陶制来得更快，成本相应较低，不仅适应死者家人单独定制的需要，而且能成批生产进入"凶肆"买卖。但是我也注意到陶俑或三彩俑的工艺并不比石刻简单，很多人物比例准确，表情丰富，眉目传情，栩栩如生，工匠的雕塑水平绝非一般人可为，既表现了雕塑创作者的追求，也表达墓葬主人"视死如视生"的意愿，洋溢着一种只有那个时代才有的特殊气象。

　　这不仅使人怀疑雕塑制造者本身是否来自中亚西域的胡人，尽管画史上只记载过来自中亚曹国的曹仲达，是位粟特人出身的画家，但是他创作的衣纹飘举、肌体贴水的"曹家样"，曾经从北齐流传至唐代，对中国图像艺术产生过重大影响。因此，我们一直猜测胡人形象的陶俑雕塑极有可能是"自画像"，应是东迁入华的西域画工、雕工、刻工、塑工等人的作品，他们将自己汲取西方的工艺创作直接带入中原内地，不仅利用舶来的手工技艺周游两京、活跃于各地，而且授艺传徒，移植技法，绘制神像，用不同的艺术手段，掀起了一股股胡化的风潮，正是浸淫在这种从工匠制作到艺术创作的文化氛围下，唐代的墓葬陶俑中才会出现那么多生动地胡人形象、昆仑奴形象和其他民族人物的形象。

　　胡人俑在中国墓葬中确切出现的时间，一直是一个疑问。我们所见大概是东汉时期随着早期佛教传入开始陆续出现一些胡人粗糙形象，沂南、徐州、武昌、四川等地零星分布。北魏时随着"五胡入华"民族融汇局面大盛，面貌清晰的胡人俑也陆续面世。北朝胡人俑形象虽然还较为笨拙粗陋，但不乏出现精品佳作。经过隋唐之际的转折，胡人艺术形象步步逼真进步很快，贵族

华美生活面貌取代了以前甲骑具装军事装束，到盛唐时期人物刻画已经非常准确到位了，并且各地出现的胡俑造型也不雷同，相对来说北方的胡俑精雕细刻，神形兼备，南方的胡俑比较粗糙，轮廓失真，其中陕西、河南、山西、甘肃等外来移民迁徙地与聚集地的胡人形象造型水平最高，有些胡俑不拘格套，雍容大气，甚至敷彩描金，推崇新奇。

对乾陵陪葬墓群中出土的胡人俑，我长期做过仔细观察，比如1960年永泰公主墓出土彩绘俑中至少有三例胡人俑曾经使人困惑不解：

1. 永泰公主墓出土的胡人袒腹俑（见本书页146），头发中分盘辫于脑后，高鼻深目，昂首上视。身穿深绿色齐膝盖皮袍，褐色绒毛里外露，绿色窄腿裤，赭色尖头靴。原来有人以为是握拳牵驼俑或牵马俑，实际注意他的手势神气十足是亮相表演状，与牵拉牲畜无关。但长期被人们误认为是牵马俑，经过多年合并同类俑系列考察，结合历史文献记载，我曾指出这类袒腹俑应是隋唐时期变幻魔术的西域幻人形象（《中国历史文物》2007年第4期）。

2. 永泰公主墓出土的胡人骑马上身裸体俑（见本书页192），肌肉隆起，筋腱暴绷，双手举起。有人将其定为"胡人力士骑马俑"，但究竟是佛教寺院守门的力士还是角抵场上摔跤的力士，没有解释，令人怀疑。我曾认为他是一种自南北朝时就从西域入华的泼寒胡戏形象，隋唐时代每年十一月"乞寒节"胡人骏马胡服、腾逐喧噪于街衢戏乐，在齐集列阵、豪歌狂舞时往往裸露身体，唐诗张说《苏幕遮》五首记有泼寒胡戏情景，但由于是独俑孤证，没有见过其他类似俑，一直不敢轻率地下结论肯定。

3. 永泰公主墓出土的另一个胡人骑马俑（见本书页184），虬髯满腮，头戴四檐毡帽，鞍座后携带圆卷物品；与斯坦因在于阗废寺丹丹乌里克木版画上发现的头戴四檐毡帽骑花斑马人物如出一辙，与北宋宫廷画师李公麟《五马图》中所绘进献于阗名马"凤头骢"的西域贡使装束非常相似，即头戴四檐毡帽；也与近年山西太原发现北齐贺拔昌墓中戴四檐毡帽胡人俑一模一样。这就说明此类胡人骑马俑很可能是西域贡使，至于是于阗贡使还是携带卷掩物件的信使，则还需要进一步研究判定。

永泰公主墓发掘已经快五十年了，我们还不能对胡人俑得出满意的解读答案，这说明并不是胡人俑一出土展示，就能说清道白，需要长期的观察对比和深入研究，望文生义的浮躁学风只能带来误读错解。尽管面对历史上许多胡人活动现在学术界还争论不休，有些甚至成为历史难题，但是我们毕竟能从胡人俑形象上可以洞察出许多重要的线索，可以包含着许多中西糅合的文化元素和历史信息。一具具胡俑呈现在我们眼前，有的造型生动，表情怪异，有的栩栩如生，毫无褪色，仿佛还带着生前的体温，依稀让人感到当时的气息，感到一种心底深藏的召唤，灵魂犹在，脊梁犹在，浮现出当年丝绸之路胡汉往来前赴后继那段岁月。

胡俑在众多人物俑中脱颖而出，在于当时艺术工匠汲取社会前沿的反映与普受关注的遴选，不断潜心追求艺术创新的表现，各类胡俑造型不是袭故蹈常，而是时尚价值的延伸。当然，更是受到不同社会阶层的欣赏喜爱和鼎力支持，才会使胡俑大大涌现。我们看到的不完全是艺术虚构的结晶，也有历史的总结和见证，或是丝路东西

六十一蕃臣石像 唐 乾陵陵园

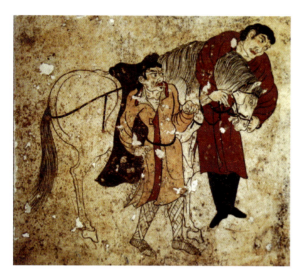

胡人备马图 唐 陕西省礼泉县韦贵妃墓出土

方艺术交流的国家形象。胡人俑写实与写意的统一表现手法，只有在唐代作为标志性雕塑佳品留给后世，堪称我国几千年历史上为数不多的朝代。

从八世纪开始，唐俑急剧减少，生动的胡人俑形象也开始慢慢消失了，甚至连穿胡服形象的女俑也很难找到了，零星的随葬陶俑形貌日显委琐，人物造型顿失盛世风貌，这与时代社会逐步走向封闭保守有关，缺失了外来文化的内涵和个性，人们眼界逐渐狭小，局限自赏自怜，优秀的雕塑创造没有了神奇的想象力，缺少胡人造型与意象的"亮点"，劲吹了几个世纪的外来风终告停息。

三

胡人、胡风、胡音对中国汉唐之间的社会产生了激烈撞击，来自外域的胡姓移民分布四方，他们的活动成为欧亚历史中最重要的篇章之一，其中遗留至今最精彩诱人的形象，我们认为就是不断出土的各种造型胡人俑，这是活生生的历史见证。

对胡人俑的系统研究，西方学者早已着手进行，20世纪20～30年代他们就大量购买中国的陶俑秘密运出国境，然后分类整理。1959年罗马曾出版了Jane Gaston Mahler（马珍妮）的《唐俑

中的西域人》专著，1998年E．Knauer女士《骆驼的生死驮载——汉唐陶俑的图像和观念及其与丝路贸易的关系》曾获得法兰西金石铭文学院"儒莲奖"。国外还有一些以"深目高鼻"为识别族属的论文陆续发表。我国在上个世纪50年代配合基本建设中将出土的胡人俑列入唐俑之中也曾有过出版，但黑白图版模糊不清，印制质量粗糙简单，只有出土地点寥寥数语，所涉内容仅在前言中稍做提及，并没有系统的研究胡人俑专题论著问世，一些本该由中国学者作出判断的重大课题，却都停滞下来一搁几十年。

近年随着考古发现的胡人形象，日积月累，不断丰富，可供人们欣赏和评论的"胡化"文物也在许多博物馆频频亮相，外国有东亚艺术的大博物馆亦不断陈列展出胡人陶俑。然而，专门针对胡人俑的研究课题很少得到资助，科研人员还没有及时跟上形成研究梯队，展览陈列里张冠李戴、胡汉不分的事情屡屡出现，所出图书中对胡人俑被选用为墓葬里凸显艺术形象探讨不深，有些谈胡说著的文章只是重复叙述，更没有从简单的艺术描述上升到对历史文明的考察体认。我遇到的具体问题就有多例，这里略举三例：

例如昆仑奴俑长期被认为是来自非洲的黑人，竟很少有人提出怀疑，有些甚至被误导到几乎完全"失声"的状态。对黑人俑的研究，文物界和学术界目前新的求证凤毛麟角，竟使人产生一锤定音的感觉。七、八年前我曾写过《唐长安黑人来源寻踪》一文，依据考古文物和唐宋史料从不同角度考证，指出当时的黑人不是来自非洲，而是来自南海诸地域，即今天的东南亚和南亚一带，文章发表后曾被多家学术报刊媒体作为新观点转摘介绍，目的就是为了纠正人们的错误认识。

又例如我们今天所能见到的唐代胡人女性俑非常罕见，当时胡姬、胡旋女等外来女性在史书文字和出土文献中都记录不少，但遗憾的是考古文物中却很难找到"胡女"，似乎只有西安出土金乡县主墓里的一个"胡女"特例，但她脸部面

容模糊不清，也绝不是唐诗上描写的胡姬，而是一个伺候女墓主的家人或女仆。这种反差值得我们注意与反思。唐人范摅撰《云溪友议》中记载桂林有胡人女子踪迹，《全唐诗》卷八百七十记载陆岩梦《桂州筵上赠胡女子》诗："自道风流不可攀，却堪蹙额更颦颜。眼睛深似湘江水，鼻孔高于华岳山。舞态固难居掌上，歌声应不绕梁间。孟阳死后欲千载，犹有佳人觅往还。"这个胡人女子深目高鼻，应当是自西域入华辗转至唐桂林寄居者。有此戏谑诗歌固然难得，唯胡人女俑在国内还是发现极少，盼望有朝一日能有新的胡人女俑图像公布。

还例如唐代胡人俑服饰装束非常引人注目，如梳辫盘髻、卷发虬髯、高尖蕃帽、翻领衣袍、小袖细衫、尖勾锦靴、葡萄飘带、玉石腰带等等，都在陶俑塑刻中表现得淋漓尽致。时尚是社会变化的缩影，服装的流行趋势是随着社会在不停的变化，胡人服装对汉人的影响肯定是这一时期胡人进入中原社会后的融入结果。特别是唐代流行的"女扮男装"俑或是"女穿胡服"俑均是当时社会风俗表现的特征，唐高宗、武则天时期还扩散成时髦装束之一，而穿着胡服的唐人俑与戴着幞头的胡人俑也比比皆是，证明了文化交流是双向的渠道。需要指出的是，尽管唐代青年女性袒胸露乳形象有所出现，服饰"洋化"，妆扮华贵，但并不是要学习西方雕塑表现身体曲线，或是突出引目勾魂的性感，而是自我意识较强，显示青春的活力，区别于步履维艰的老妇。这也是其他朝代很难出现的艺术表现。

我始终认为，千年前长安、洛阳等丝路胡风能够留下的映象，主要就是这些幻影般定格的胡人俑，犹如一首送给一座消逝城市的视觉挽歌。如果说，唐人在安史之乱前似乎较少排挤外来的胡人，通过陵墓中陪葬的胡人俑凸显了这一实事，那么这种趋势在中唐以后继续延续则愈来愈少了。各地出土陶俑表现的是大历史中的小细节，有些胡人武俑体格健壮丰盈，有些卖艺胡人表情生动活泼，有的线条浑圆饱满，有的神态昂

扬自若，但正是细节才真正让历史变得血肉丰满，经络俱全，让人们记住历史遗产而有了追溯的价值与怀旧的共鸣。假如缺少胡俑这些细节，历史就只是一个模糊的轮廓，历史是由生活构成的，生活无往而不在历史之中，那些透过生活细节看到的历史也往往更可信。

实际上，胡人俑惟妙惟肖的形象背后有许多世人莫知的隐秘，"探秘"需要大历史视野下的中西交流史眼光，通过两种异质文化互相接纳，通过细致繁密的考证尽可能接触当时一些见证人的记载。我不愿在彩绘陶俑和三彩俑的质地材料区别上做过多分析，无论是唐初的陶或是高宗时期出现的瓷，皆有精湛作品，我们更关注的是人物造型所赋予的社会意义，丰富多彩的千年胡人俑走出地下舒展着自己的生命，出现在我们面前的是一段记忆犹新的活的历史，会使我们研究更加具体化、形象化，值得更多人来参与关注，以文物填补历史的空白页。

胡人俑是雕塑艺术中的一个独特的造型，而艺术恰恰是人类一种重要的沟通工具，能够使不同民族走到一起来，从相识、相知到相互理解和尊重。陶俑雕塑为历史提供了不可磨灭的证据，是古代"纪实塑造"的凝固影像，是当时历史进程中的艺术积淀和人物见证，是最能使人信服的记录和文物意象。我们研究胡人俑并策划举办展览，并不是热衷于种族的寻根，回归胡汉交融传统，也不是考证有趣史实，单纯追忆过去上千年的历史，而是透过胡俑展览启发人们思考人类交往中的双向理解，共同关注未来创造的生活，包含着我们今天的对外开放与融入世界。

我们相信这次胡俑展一定会圆满成功，并祝愿它能走向丝绸之路沿途各国巡展或者"特别展出"，因为唤醒千年胡俑的性灵，再现外来文明的画卷，分享祖先的艺术成果，是现代人们应该承担的责任。胡人俑是全世界文化遗产的一种艺术造型载体，也是全人类值得共同记忆的一段历史。

The Silk Road and the Terracotta Foreigners of the Tand Dynasty

◎ By Ge Chengyong

The exhibition of terracotta foreigners held by the Museum of Qianling Mausoleum is the first special concentrative one around the world, the images on display, moreover, are the foreigners with Roman nose, deep-set eyes or sideburns described in the Tang poems. The topic is the Silk Road and the exchanges between China and foreign countries. In recent years, many terracotta foreigners have unearthed in the tombs of the Northern Dynasties and the Sui and Tang Dynasties, so they are familiar and attractive to the people.

By extraordinary craftsmanship, the terracotta makers filled the puppets with living soul and featured it with vivid foreign looks, which reflects the artistic form and a real historical life of that time. According to the historical records of the Tang Dynasty, the immigrants from Central Asia resided in the Western Region and entered into Proper China through the Silk Road. They made their living by trade, livestock raising, farming, wine-selling or acrobatic show. Some of them were attendants, while others were officials in the government of the Tang Dynasty.

The marriage between foreigners and the people of Han made their offspring half-breeds with mixed facial characters. As the most ancient Indo-European race in Central Asia, the people there kept marriage relationship with Turks, hence the national unification made it difficult to judge their origins only by appearance. Because of this unsolved anthropological problem, many attempts in identifying the terracotta foreigners seem to be fruitless efforts. The terracotta foreigners provide access to the study of the Western Region and other nationalities, but misunderstanding occurs easily if we simply make judgement depending on their facial features.

The terracotta foreigners show different social classes, but most of them are slaves. They are attendants of the tomb owners in underworld. Now, it is unable to imagine the inner world and real condition of these slaves, but we can still be sensible of their tragic fate from the layout of the terracotta foreigners in tombs.

As visual cultural works, the terracotta foreigners are substitutes placed in the wall niche or tomb chamber. They belong to the special symbolic space constructed for the dead, and their images, in a sense, are living. Despite of the individual forms, each of the terracotta foreigners is a necessary part of the funerary ware. There are 770 terracotta figurines in the tomb of Princess Yongtai, 905 pieces in the tomb of Prince Yide, and 600 in the tomb of Prince Zhanghuai. The vast quantity and scale of the terracotta figurines show a high artistic level and the great superiority of the royal family. In them, the images of foreigner are not as great in amount.

It is interesting to find a synthetic application of realistic and imagery expression in the terracotta figurines' creation. The whole body of the terracotta figurines in one tomb consists of various themes or groups including musicians, acrobats, officials, parades of armed forces, attendants and hunters, and the foreigners often can be found in each group. Their existence in the tombs symbolizes the obedience and submission of other nations to China, and the tomb owners' luxurious lives last eternally in the Underworld.

Perhaps, the craftsmen themselves were from Central Asia. They introduced west style into China, prompting waves of exotic flavor. Under such cultural atmosphere could these vivid terracotta foreigners be made.

It is suspended when the first terracotta foreigners appeared in China, but some coarse images already emerged as the spread of Buddhism during the Eastern Han Dynasty. Its skill developed in the Northern Dynasties and became more exquisite in the Tang Dynasty. Relatively speaking, the terracotta foreigners made in North China, especially the residential areas of immigrants such as Shanxi, Henan, Gansu etc., were better than the ones made in South China.

It has been 50 years since the excavation of the tomb of Princess Yongtai initiated, there is room for improvement in the research of terracotta foreigners yet. Detailed comparison and further analysis are essential to our comprehension. Indeed, the terracotta foreigners offer us vital information, and their appealing images remind us of those immigrants traveled through the Silk Road. The terracotta foreigners of Tang were carried forward as symbolic artworks. The ones produced later, however, generally lost their charm for the conservative trend in Chinese society and lack of nutrition by foreign culture.

Foreign customs imposed great impact onto the societies from the Han to the Tang Dynasties. The immigrants in China played an important role in the Euro-Asian history. Undoubtedly, the terracotta foreigners function as witness to the past.

As to the systematic research on the terracotta foreigners, western scholars started earlier, especially the famous monographies published by Jane Gaston Mahler and E. Knauer respectively in 1959 and 1998. On the contrary, Chinese academic circle made a slow response on this topic. Though more and more cultural relics related to the foreigners in ancient China have unearthed in recent years, more attention and further consideration on them are required. I want to point out: 1. The terracotta Kunlun slaves were modeled on the black men who were not from Africa, but from South-east Asia or South Asia. 2. We should pay attention to a sharp contrast that the terracotta foreign women are rare comparing to the richness of historical materials on them. 3. The terracotta Chinese girls were dressed in west fashion in order to show their energy of youth, not for sexy seducement.

The terracotta foreigners reflect the exotic customs ever permeated in Chang'an and Luoyang of the Tang Dynasty. We know from them that the people of Tang hardly discriminated against the foreigners before the An Lushan Rebellion, and this attitude was kept for a long time after the middle period of Tang. As a part of history, the terracotta foreigners open a window for us to seek the historical truth.

Actually, in order to solve the mysteries behind these vivid terracotta foreigners, we have to study carefully on the first-hand materials with a perspective of the exchanges between China and foreign countries. We should attach more importance to the social significance of the terracotta foreigners instead of their materials.

The terracotta foreigner is a special case of the sculptural art, while art is a communication tool making different races understand each other. The terracotta figures are convincing evidences for historical research. Our exhibition is not for tracing their origins or simply memorizing the past, but for enlightening the consideration on the mutual effects of human communication and inviting concerns on the future life.

唐代胡俑的出土和分类

◎ 乾陵博物馆

　　"胡人"是我国古代对北方边地及西域各族的称呼。若"胡"、"汉"并提，即视"胡"为"非汉人"的话，则其范围要宽泛得多。那些曾在中原地区建立王朝，如建立北朝政权的拓拔鲜卑族亦应在其列。因此，我们特地对唐代胡俑文物展的对象做了限定，将其缩小为古代中国西部和西北部的各族。

　　因"胡"所牵涉的民族之广，造成胡俑形象之异。这使得判定胡人俑的族属成为一个难题。学界至今还未能将中古时期上述地区的民族与境内所出胡人俑的族属一一对应起来。

　　在探讨唐代"胡人"相关问题时，为了避免概念上的枝节出入，有的学者高度概括地归结为"'胡人'形象"。视"深目高鼻"以及穿戴与当时汉族不同衣冠为"胡人"的外在特征（刘文锁《唐代'胡人'图像初探》，《欧亚学刊》2007年第6辑），并将胡人图像题材划分为绘画（壁画、绢画和其它）和雕塑（陶或三彩俑、石刻、金银器、砖、玉雕、尊形器等）两大类。若此，"'胡人'图像"的内涵要远比"胡俑"来得大。

　　"胡俑"主要作为墓葬的陪葬品，其质地多为陶质，包括釉陶的唐三彩，也有石质、瓷质等。胡俑在出土或传世文物中皆有之，成为学者关注的一个重要课题。较早涉及的论著有：向达先生的《唐代长安与西域文明》、沈从文先生的《中国古代服饰研究》和美国哥伦比亚大学Jane Caston Mahler的《唐俑中的西域人》。近年来，对胡人图像特别是胡俑文物有较深研究的论著主要有：孙机先生的《中国圣火》、葛承雍先生的《唐韵胡音与外来文明》、荣新江先生的粟特史研究系列著作如《中古中国与外来文明》、《从撒马尔罕到长安——粟特人在中国的文化遗迹》，以及齐东方先生的《唐代金银器研究》、《隋唐考古》等。而对唐代胡俑曾做过专题研究的有任江、刘文锁等学者。据悉，美国的迈克先生近年正对海外中国胡俑的资料进行系统的收集、整理。而著录有"胡俑"的图录或者论证中言及"胡俑"的论著较多，此不赘举。

　　作为文物中陶瓷器大类中的一个子目，当"胡俑"一词被考古和历史工作者广泛使用时，可能会产生一个误解：胡俑文物总量很大，胡俑在一个墓葬中的比例较高。实际情况并非如此。当我们确定展览内容，着手收集资料，进行文物统计、比例调查时，逐渐形成如下四点感受。第一，胡俑文物的总量并不多。虽然唐代胡俑在陕西、河南、甘肃、山西、宁夏、江苏、河北、湖北、云南、新疆、重庆、吉林、黑龙江、辽宁等省、市、自治区都有发现，但数量并不多。如，陕西历史博物馆藏品中的精品胡俑（包括乾陵陪葬墓的胡俑）不超过40件，而西安博物院馆藏胡俑文物也不足30件。这种现象应该与胡人在唐朝充当的社会角色紧密相关。第二，胡俑出土相对比较集中，主要出土于唐代的几个权力中心。首先，唐代两京地区的皇室贵族墓是出土胡俑最为集中之处，其中长安地区胡俑又多见于关中唐陵的陪葬墓。其次，是地处多民族杂居、古代丝绸之路要道的陇右。再次，是唐王朝的北方门户太原周围。而其它地区的胡俑则出土数量不大，且较分散。第三，各地胡俑各有特色。若从造型上看，以昭陵和乾陵陪葬墓出土的胡俑最为特殊，体量也较大；从保存完整性上看，以甘肃秦安县出土的一批胡俑的色彩、纹饰最可宝贵；而洛阳胡俑亦别具特色，给人色彩亮丽柔和，制作精工细腻的感觉。第四，就胡俑文物所占各个墓葬文物比例看，并不高。以乾陵为例，总共4300多件文物中，典型的深目高鼻胡俑文物却不及30件。昭陵胡俑所占比例则更少。这两处唐陵陪葬墓随葬品都是劫后余存，如果考虑到这种不完整性，则胡俑实际所占明器的比例还要更低一些。

在省文物局的关照下，我们在对陕西胡俑文物进行初步了解后，在全省范围内借调胡俑。陕西历史博物馆、陕西考古研究院、咸阳市文物局、宝鸡市文物局、渭南市文物局、西安博物院给予大力协助，共调来97件胡俑支援我馆陈列工作。这些胡俑大部分造型优美，而且相当一部分是尚未发表的。如，陕西考古研究院借调的31件胡俑；渭南文物局从蒲城县调来的桥陵陪葬墓出土的10余件胡俑，不仅体量较大，也都没有正式发表展示过。在此，我们要对友邻单位的鼎力支持表示由衷的感谢。

为了较为全面地展示唐代胡人的风采，我们在有限的陈列空间，选取120件文物作为实体展品。另外，采用多媒体和数字技术，尽可能地展示与唐代胡人有关的各种图像，包括壁画、陶及三彩胡俑形象；同时，尽可能多地展示与胡俑有关的文献碑碣资料，包括正史记载和出土墓志。

为了保证胡俑陈列的科学性和学术成果展示的前沿性，我们先后召开四次学术座谈会，诚邀专家学者为陈列内容、主题思想及展览艺术性献计献策。著名文物研究专家孙机、杨泓先生，以及在民族史和中外文化交流史研究领域颇具声望的周伟洲、葛承雍、李鸿宾、扬之水、荣新江、杨希义、齐东方诸先生，在博物馆和唐史领域具有影响的马振智、张建林、秦建明、赵力光、张礼智、王世平、沈睿文、姜捷、孔正一、韩建武、谢伟等先生，都为本次陈列提出了自己的灼见。

尊重学者意见，依据文物特点，我们将陈列分为魅力大唐、丝路灵魂、乐居长安和胡风东渐四个部分，本书文物编排也按照陈列内容分为四个小节，因而没有按照时代和墓葬、质地分类。

此次展览是为配合陕西省申遗工作而展开，同时是陕西省文物局迎接奥运会的项目。作为国内外第一次系统展示唐代胡人风采，旌扬胡人对唐代文明形成和发展所起的积极作用，本展览受到省局领导、业内人士和社会各界的高度关注，随此机缘编印出版本书，也成为势之所至。文物出版社总编辑葛承雍先生不仅为胡俑陈列工作四处奔忙，也为本书的编辑呕心沥血。孙机先生和杨泓先生的宏论美文，无疑是本书的灵魂所在。

目前，国内外对唐代胡俑的研究尚嫌薄弱，而我馆业务人员对胡俑的研究水平有限。书中错讹之处，敬祈指陈。

Excavation and Classification of the Terracotta Foreigners of the Tang Dynasty

◎ By the Museum of Qianling Mausoleum

Huren is an appellation given by ancient Chinese to the ethnic nationalities of China's northern frontier and western region. If Hu and Han are mentioned together, the term of Hu would include all the non-Han ethnic groups. Huren in this book refers to the peoples of the ethnic groups in west and northwest China during the Tang times. Since Huren were composed of several ethnic groups, it is difficult to determine the exact ethnicity of each Hu figurine (Huyong). So far scholars in the field are not very successful in figuring out a proper match between the ethnic groups living in the above-mentioned regions during the medieval times and the Hu figurines found in these regions. Some scholars believe that "deep eyes", "high-bridged nose", and different dressing style are external features of Hu people and they therefore divide the theme of the Hu images into two categories of painting and sculpture. The Hu figurines are an important component of this theme.

As funerary articles, most of Hu figurines were made of pottery and some were made of stone and porcelain. Among the unearthed or handed-down antiques, there are a number of Hu figurines, and this makes their study an important academic subject. The earlier works on this subject include Xiang Da's Tangdai Chang'an yu Xiyu wenming(Chang'an and the Civilization of the Western Regions in the Tang Dynasty), Shen Congwen's Zhongguo gudai fushi yanjiu (Studies on Ancient Chinese Costumes), and The Westerners among the Figurines of the T'ang Dynasty of China by Jane Gaston Mahler of Columbia University. More recent works on the Hu images, especially on figurines, include Sun Ji's Zhongguo shenghuo (The Sacred Fire of China), Ge Chengyong's Tangyu Huyin yu wailai wenming (Tang Rhyme, Hu Melody and Foreign Civilization), Rong Xinjiang's Zhonggu Zhongguo yu Wailai wenming (Medieval China and Foreign Civilization), Cong Sama'erhan dao Chang'an: Suteren zai Zhongguo de wenhua yiji (From Samarkand to Chang'an: Cultural Remains of the Sogdians in China), as well as Qi Dongfang's Tangdai jinyinqi yanjiu (Studies on Tang Gold and Silver Wares), and Sui Tang kaogu (Archaeological Studies on Sui and Tang Dynasties). Focused studies on Hu figurines were also conducted by Ren Jiang and Liu Wensuo and many others. As far as we know, there is at least one American scholar who is working on a systematic collection and collation of the overseas materials of the Chinese Hu figurines.

In recent years, the term Huyong has been widely used by archaeologists and historians, which led to a popular misconception that there is a large quantity of Hu figurines and they account for a high percentage in the total funerary articles in any Tang tomb. This is not true. In the course of our studying on Hu figurines, several points have come to be clear. First, the total amount of Hu figurines is not plenty. Although Tang dynasty Hu figurines were discovered in many regions including Shaanxi, Henan, Gansu, Shanxi, Ningxia, Jiangsu, Hebei, Hubei, Yunnan, Xinjiang, Chongqing, Jilin, Heilongjiang, and Liaoning, the number in each region is not large. For instance, the Hu figurines collected by Shaanxi History Museum are no more than forty, and there are less than thirty in Xi'an Museum. This phenomenon might be related to the social role played by Hu people during the Tang dynasty. Second, the areas where Hu figurines were discovered are relatively concentrated. The most intensive distribution was found first in the tombs of aristocrats and officials in the (Tang) capital areas of Chang'an and Luoyang, and next in the multi-ethnic mixed area in eastern Gansu, and then in the vicinity of Taiyuan. In the other areas, the number of the unearthed Hu figurines is small and sporadic. Third, the style of Hu figurines from various regions is different. In terms of mold form, the most special ones come from Zhao Tomb and Qian Tomb. In terms of preservation quality, the most precious ones are those unearthed from Qin'an county of Gansu for their color and ornamentation. The figurines discovered in Luoyang also have some extra traits with their bright and soft color as well as exquisite handcraft art. Fourth, the percentage of Hu figurines in each tomb's funeral articles is low. Take Qian Tomb for example. Among the 4,300 pieces of antiques unearthed, the Hu figurines of typical "deep eyes and high-bridged nose" are less than thirty. This percentage is even lower than that in Zhao Tomb. Considering the incompleteness of the burial articles caused by grave robberies to these two tombs, the actual percentage of the Hu figurines in the whole mingqi (spirit articles) might be even lower.

In order to cooperate with Shaanxi's "World Heritage" application as well as to welcome the 2008 Beijing Olympic Games, we decided to hold the "Exhibition of the Tang Dynasty Hu Figurines". With the help of the provincial Cultural Relics Bureau, we conducted a comprehensive survey on the Hu figurine relics, and temporarily transferred all the available Hu figurines in various parts of Shaanxi (to the exhibition cite). We received active cooperation from Shaanxi History Museum, Shaanxi Provincial Academy of Archaeology, Cultural Relics Bureaus of Xianyang, Baoji and Weinan, and Xi'an Museum. We managed to transfer ninety-seven Hu figurines for this exhibition from them. Most of these figurines are gracefully styled and are of highly historical and artistic value. Many of them have never been publicly displayed previously. For example, the thirty-one figurines from Shaanxi Provincial Academy of Archaeology and over ten figurines borrowed from Pucheng County by the Cultural Relics Bureau of Weinan have never been formally shown in public in the past.

Due to the limited display space, we carefully selected one hundred and twenty pieces of antiques as the entire exhibits. With the support of the multimedia and digital technology, we made our best effort to display all kinds of images related to the Tang dynasty Hu people, including fresco, pottery and tri-colored glazed Hu figurines. At the same time, we also displayed the documental and epigraphic materials about Hu figurines as many as possible, including the official historical records and the unearthed epitaphs. To guarantee the scientificalness and accuracy of the pioneering academic findings on the displayed Hu figurines, we successively held four symposiums and sought advice from specialists on the display content, theme, and art. Many noted scholars, including Sun Ji, Yang Hong, Zhou Weizhou, Ge Chengyong, Li Hongbin, Yang Zhishui, Rong Xinjiang, Yang Xiyi, Qi Dongfang, Ma Zhenzhi, Zhang Jianlin, Qin Jianming, Zhao Liguang, Zhang Lizhi, Wang Shiping, Shen Ruiwen, Jiang Jie, Kong Zhengyi, Han Jianwu and Xie Wei, made a valuable contribution to this exhibition by giving their opinions and suggestions.

Following advice from various experts, we decided to divide our exhibits into four sections according to their characteristics: the Attractions of the Great Tang, the Spirit of the Silk Road, the Guests in Chang'an, and the Eastward Spread of Hu Culture. This exhibition is the first public display of the Tang dynasty Hu people, which aims to publicize and highlight their active contribution to the formation and development of the Tang civilization. This exhibition has received great attention from the provincial leaders, our peers, and people of all walks of life. The publication of Tangdai Huyong (The Tang Dynasty Hu Figurines) is a natural outcome of this event. The book is divided into four chapters in accordance with the display content, instead of chronicle order, tomb type and texture classification. Mr. Ge Chengyong, the editor-in-chief of the Cultural Relics Publishing House, not only worked hard on the display, but also contributed significantly to the editing of the book. Mr. Sun Ji and Yang Hong's advice and writings have greatly enhanced the scholarly value of the book. We would also like to offer sincere thanks to those friendly museums that provide us with the figurines on display, to all the specialists who attended our symposiums, to our colleagues at the Cultural Relics Publishing House, and to the scholars who contributed articles to this book.

Being the material evidence of the cultural exchange of the Tang dynasty, the Hu figurines have high research value. Currently, the research on the Tang dynasty Hu figurine is still in its initial stage both in China and overseas. Many issues are waiting to be solved. Limited by the level of our knowledge, our research on Hu figurines might be insufficient and flawed. Your comment on and critique of the book are sincerely appreciated.

专题文章
Articles

公元618年，唐王朝建立，

中国封建社会进入又一鼎盛时期。

唐疆域辽阔，国力强盛，经济繁荣，文化昌盛，

对外交流频繁，都城长安成为国际化大都市。

来自外国和西域地区政权的

使节、僧侣、留学生、商人、艺人等络绎不绝，

这些人就是唐代典籍中所记载的"胡人"。

以胡人形象为蓝本所烧造的陶俑，

被考古学家称为"胡俑"。

历年来，地下出土的多姿多彩的唐代胡俑，

成为反映唐时期胡人在京畿地区活动的实物见证。

《丝路胡人外来风——唐代胡俑展》的举办，

是将陕西1949年以来出土的胡俑精品

和近年新出土珍贵文物集中陈列，

展示以丝绸之路为主线的国际文化交流背景下

胡人在长安的活动状况，

彰显其为唐文化的形成与发展所做出的积极贡献，

揭示文化交流与民族融合

在历史文明发展过程中的促进作用。

第一单元 魅力大唐

唐代的对外开放与胡俑出土

Charm of the Tang Dynasty: Opening-up and the Excavation of Terracotta Foreigners

　　全国各地出土的胡俑充分反映了唐王朝开放进取、和谐万邦的时代特征。胡俑的出土地，主要集中在以唐长安城为中心，西起天水，东到潼关的渭水流域，其中以昭陵与乾陵陪葬墓出土数量最多。此外，东都洛阳与扬州、广州等几个唐朝的商业中心和丝绸之路沿线城镇也出土了不少胡俑。从已知资料看，胡俑的出土也沿丝路分布。而我们所熟悉的昭陵、乾陵石刻是胡人形象的集中体现。

唐三彩胡人骑驼俑

高76、宽25、长51厘米
陕西省礼泉县唐昭陵陪葬墓出土
现藏陕西昭陵博物馆

Figurine of three-color glazed ceramic Hu camel rider

76cm high, 25 cm wide, 51cm long
Excavated from the accompanying tomb of Zhaoling of Tang
dynasty in Liquan County, Shaanxi
Housed at Zhaoling Museum of Shaanxi

唐三彩胡人俑

高44、宽13、厚12厘米
陕西省礼泉县唐昭陵02号墓出土
现藏陕西昭陵博物馆

Figurine of three-color glazed ceramic Hu man

44cm high, 13cm wide, 12cm thick
Excavated from no. 2 tomb of Zhaoling of Tang dynasty in
Liquan County，Shaanxi
Housed at Zhaoling Museum of Shaanxi

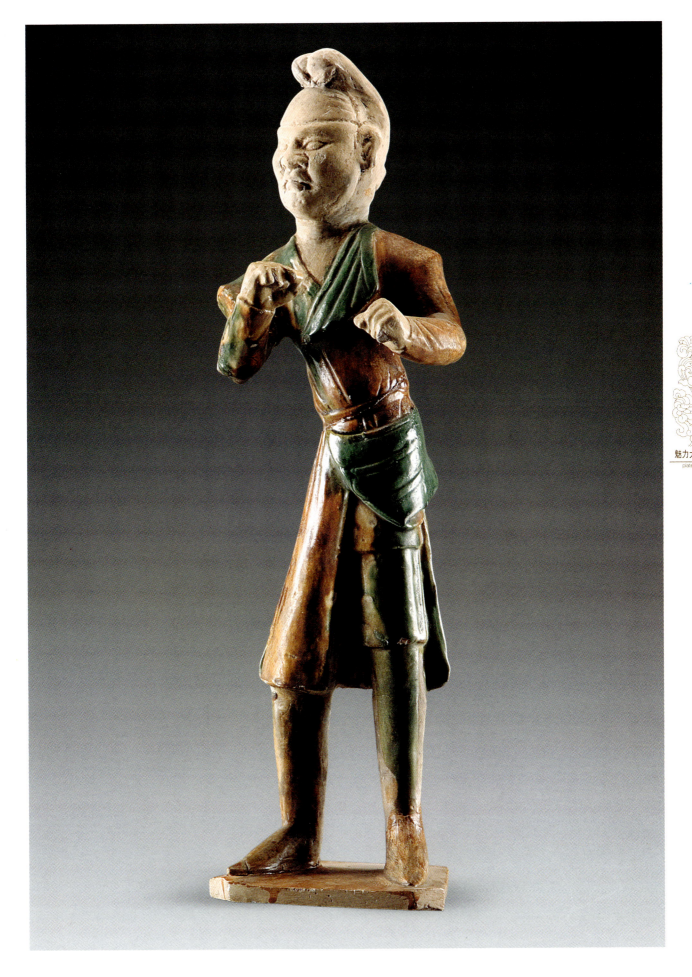

唐黄釉绿领胡俑

高22.8厘米
1972年河南省洛阳市涧西区矿山厂出土
现藏河南省洛阳市博物馆

Figurine of yellow-glazed ceramic Hu man with green-collar

22.8cm high
Unearthed in Kuangshanchang, Jianxi District, Luoyang, Henan, 1972
Housed at Luoyang Museum of Henan

唐三彩胡人俑

高49厘米
1972年河南省洛阳市郊区车圪垱出土
现藏河南省洛阳市博物馆

Figurine of three-color glazed ceramic Hu man

49cm high
Unearthed in Chegedang, suburb of Luoyang, Henan, 1972
Housed at Luoyang Museum of Henan

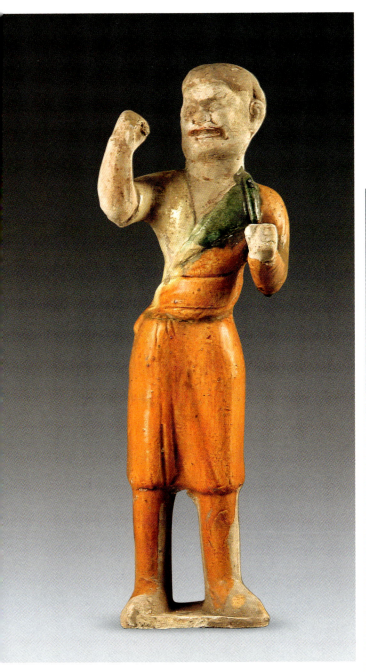

唐三彩胡人俑

高45厘米

1972年河南省洛阳市涧西区矿山厂出土

Figurine of three-color glazed ceramic Hu man

45cm high
Unearthed in Kuangshanchang, Jianxi
District, Luoyang, Henan, 1972

唐三彩胡人俑

高43厘米

河南省洛阳市出土

Figurine of three-color glazed ceramic Hu man

43cm high
Unearthed in Luoyang, Henan

唐三彩载物骆驼

高83、宽32、长66厘米
1972年陕西省乾县唐章怀太子墓出土
现藏陕西乾陵博物馆

Figurine of three-color glazed ceramic loaded camel

83cm high, 32cm wide, 66cm long
Excavated from the tomb of Crown Prince Zhanghuai of Tang
dynasty in Qian County, Shaanxi, 1972
Housed at Qianling Museum of Shaanxi

唐陶三彩胡人俑

高60、宽21、厚21厘米
1956年陕西省西安市长安嘉里村出土
现藏陕西历史博物馆

Figurine of three-colored pottery Hu man

60cm high, 21cm wide, 21cm thick
Unearthed in Chang'an Jiali Village, Xi'an, Shaanxi, 1956
Housed at Shaanxi History Museum

唐陶彩绘胡人俑

高29.5、宽13、厚10厘米
陕西省凤翔县雍康小区出土
现藏宝鸡凤翔县博物馆

Figurine of painted pottery Hu man

29.5cm high, 13cm wide,
10cm thick
Unearthed in Yongkang District
of Fengxiang County, Shaanxi
Housed at Fengxiang Museum
of Baoji

唐三彩胡人俑

高67、宽24、厚18厘米
1972年陕西省乾县唐章怀太子
墓出土
现藏陕西乾陵博物馆

Figurine of three-color glazed ceramic Hu man

67cm high, 24cm wide, 18cm thick
Excavated from the tomb of Crown
Prince Zhanghuai of Tang dynasty
in Qian County, Shaanxi, 1972
Housed at Qianling Museum of
Shaanxi

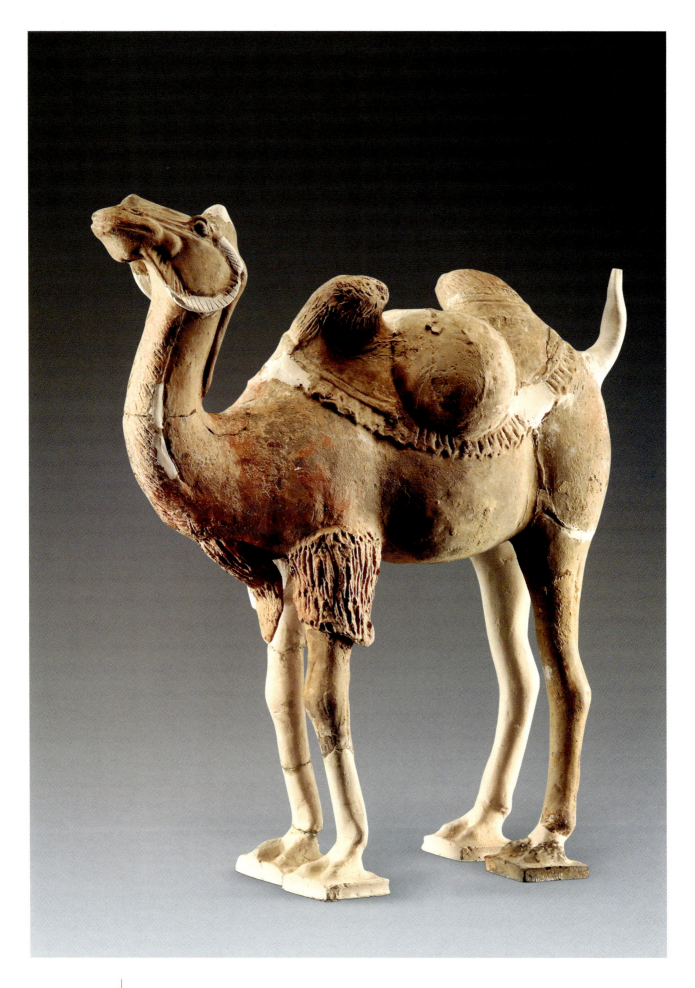

唐陶彩绘骆驼

高50、宽19、长45厘米
1972年陕西省乾县唐章怀太子墓出土
现藏陕西乾陵博物馆

Figurine of painted pottery camel

50cm high, 19cm wide, 45cm long
Excavated from the tomb of Crown Prince
Zhanghuai of Tang dynasty in Qian County,
Shaanxi, 1972
Housed at Qianling Museum of Shaanxi

唐陶彩绘胡人俑

高63.5、宽25、厚18厘米
1972年陕西省乾县唐章怀太子墓出土
现藏陕西乾陵博物馆

Figurine of painted pottery Hu man

63.5cm high, 25cm wide, 18cm thick
Excavated from the tomb of Crown Prince
Zhanghuai of Tang dynasty in Qian County,
Shaanxi, 1972
Housed at Qianling Museum of Shaanxi

唐陶彩绘胡人俑头

高15、宽8、厚9厘米
陕西省西安市西郊出土
现藏陕西历史博物馆

Figurine of painted pottery Hu man head

15cm high, 8cm wide, 9cm thick
Unearthed in the western suburb of Xi'an,
Shaanxi
Housed at Shaanxi History Museum

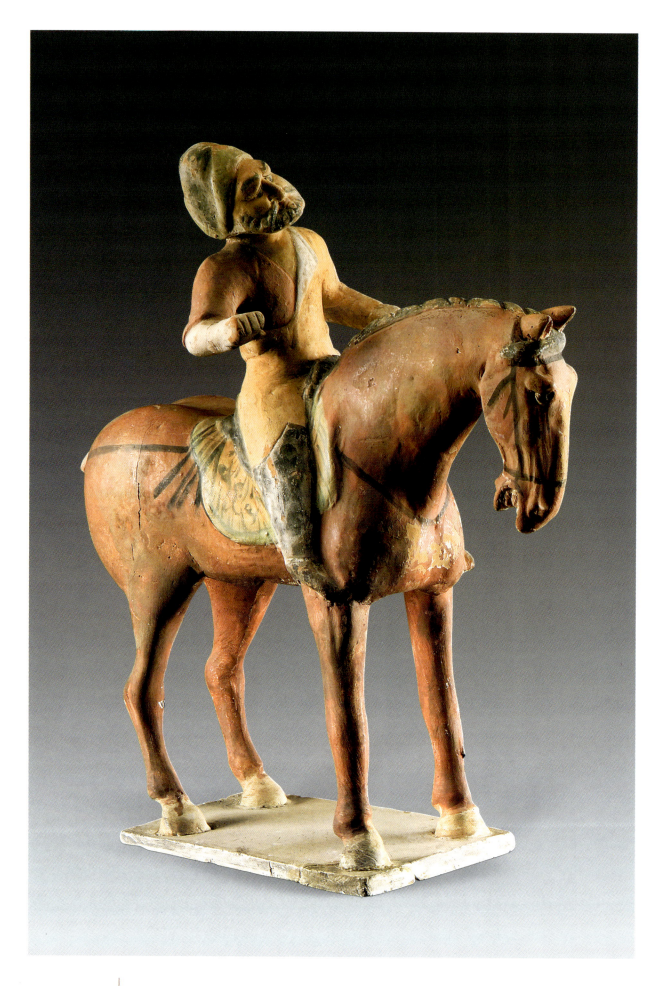

唐陶彩绘胡人骑马俑

高39、宽13、长37厘米
陕西省礼泉县唐张士贵墓出土
现藏陕西历史博物馆

Figurine of painted pottery Hu horse rider

39cm high, 13cm wide, 37cm long
Excavated from the tomb of Zhang Shigui of Tang dynasty
in Liquan County, Shaanxi
Housed at Shanxi History Museum

唐陶彩绘胡人骑马俑

高48、宽17、长42厘米
陕西省礼泉县唐韦贵妃墓出土
现藏陕西昭陵博物馆

Figurine of painted pottery Hu horse rider

48cm high, 17cm wide, 42cm long
Excavated from the tomb of Consort Wei of Tang
dynasty in Liquan County, Shaanxi
Housed at Zhaoling Museum of Shaanxi

唐陶彩绘胡人骑马俑

高30、宽10、长24厘米
1960年陕西省乾县唐永泰公主墓出土
现藏陕西乾陵博物馆

Figurine of painted pottery Hu horse rider

30cm high, 10cm wide, 24cm long
Unearthed from the tomb of Princess Yongtai of Tang
dynasty in Qian County, Shaanxi, 1960
Housed at Qianling Museum of Shaanxi

唐彩绘釉陶吹哨胡人骑马俑

高39、宽12、长23厘米
陕西省礼泉县唐郑仁泰墓出土
现藏陕西昭陵博物馆

Figurine of painted glazed ceramic Hu whistling horse rider

39cm high, 12cm wide, 23cm long
Excavated from the tomb of Zheng Rentai of Tang dynasty in Liquan County, Shaanxi
Housed at Zhaoling Museum of Shaanxi

53

唐三彩胡人俑头

高11、宽8.5、厚8厘米
现藏渭南富平县文物旅游局

Figurine of three-color glazed ceramic Hu person head

11cm high, 8.5cm wide, 8cm long
Housed at Cultural Relic and Tourism Bureau of Fuping County of Weinan

唐陶彩绘胡人半身俑

高12、宽7、厚6厘米
陕西省永寿县出土
现藏陕西咸阳文物保护中心

Figurine of painted pottery Hu man bust

12cm high, 7cm wide, 6cm thick
Unearthed in Yongshou County, Shaanxi
Housed at Xianyang Cultural Relic
Conservation Centre of Shaanxi

55

唐陶彩绘胡人跪坐俑

高14、宽8、厚6厘米
现藏陕西省考古研究院

**Figurine of painted pottery
kneeling Hu man**

14cm high, 8cm wide, 6cm thick
Housed at Shaanxi Provincial
Academy of Archaeology

唐三彩胡人俑

高45厘米
河南省洛阳市出土

Figurine of three-color glazed ceramic Hu man

45cm high
Unearthed in Luoyang, Henan

唐三彩后堕髻胡人俑

高58厘米
1963年河南省洛阳市郊区出土

Figurine of three-color glazed ceramic Hu man with falling-hair bun

58cm high
Unearthed in the suburb of Luoyang, Henan, 1963

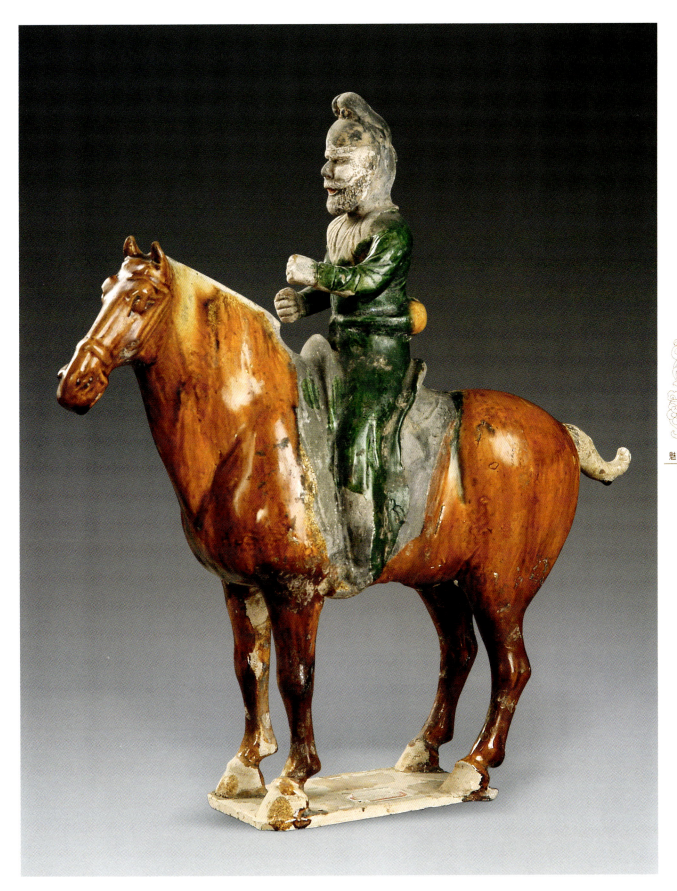

唐三彩胡人骑马俑

高41、长38.7厘米
1981年河南省洛阳市龙门东山安菩墓出土

Figurine of three-color glazed ceramic Hu horse rider

41cm high, 38.7cm long
Excavated from the tomb of Anpu in the eastern mountain of
Longmen, Luoyang, Henan, 1981

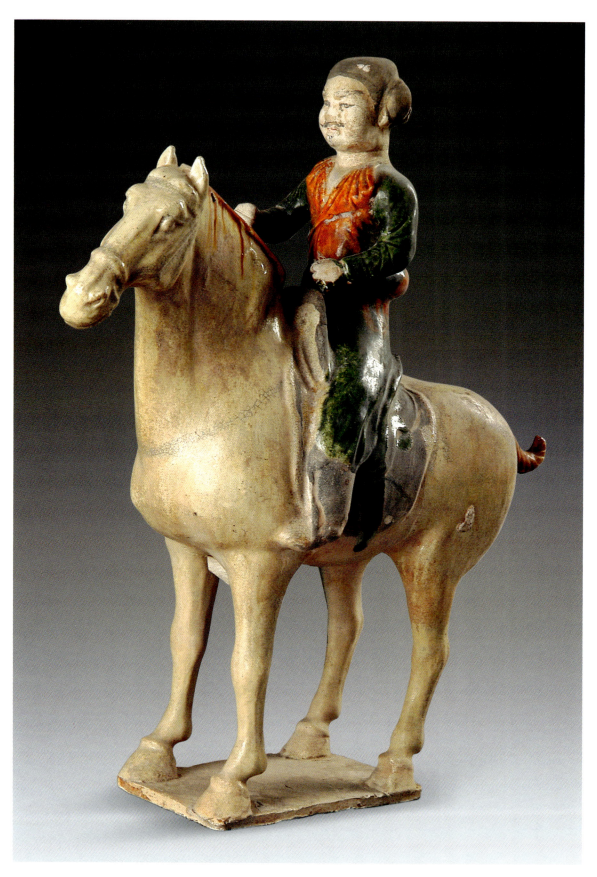

唐三彩骑马男俑

高38、长41厘米
1981年河南省洛阳市龙门东山安菩墓出土

Figurine of three-color glazed ceramic male horse rider

38cm high, 41cm long
Excavated from the tomb of Anpu in the eastern mountain of
Longmen, Luoyang, Henan, 1981

唐三彩胡俑

高26.3厘米
1999年陕西省长安县郭杜
镇出土

**Figurine of three-color
glazed ceramic Hu man**

26.3cm high
Excavated in Guodu ,Chang'an
County,Shaanxi,1999

唐三彩胡人武官俑

高49.2厘米
2002年陕西省西安市南郊唐墓出土

Figurine of Hu man

49.2cm high
Unearthed in the tomb of Tang dynasty in the southern
surburd of Xi'an,Shaanxi,2002

第二单元

丝路灵魂

唐代丝绸之路上的胡人

The Soul of the Silk Road: Immigrants on the
Silk Road of the Tang Dynasty

西汉时期贯通的丝绸之路以长安为起点，经河西走廊、新疆进入中亚、西亚地区，最后到达欧洲腹地的罗马帝国，是当时世界上东西方之间最重要的贸易和文化交流通道之一。在唐太宗和唐高宗两代帝王的精心经营下，丝绸之路畅通无阻，出现了"伊吾之右，波斯以东，商旅相继，职贡不绝"的空前繁荣景象。在所有的胡俑文物中，商人形象和表现丝路贸易情形者所占比例最高，反映了丝路经济的繁荣景象。

唐陶彩绘胡人骑驼俑

高47、宽24、长52厘米
现藏陕西省考古研究院

Figurine of painted pottery Hu camel rider

47cm high, 24cm wide, 52cm long
Housed at Shaanxi Provincial Academy of
Archaeology

唐陶彩绘胡人骑驼俑

高55、宽33、长80厘米
陕西省蒲城县唐惠陵出土
现藏渭南市蒲城县博物馆

Figurine of painted pottery Hu camel rider

55cm high, 33cm wide, 80cm long
Excavated from the tomb of Hui Tomb of Tang
dynasty in Pucheng County, Shaanxi
Housed at Pucheng Museum of Weinan

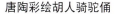

唐陶彩绘载物骆驼

高39、宽20、长38厘米
陕西省礼泉唐昭陵陪葬墓出土
现藏陕西昭陵博物馆

Figurine of painted pottery loaded camel

39cm high, 20cm wide, 38cm long
Excavated from the accompanying tomb of Zhao
Tomb of Tang dynasty in Liquan County, Shaanxi
Housed at Zhaoling Museum of Shaanxi

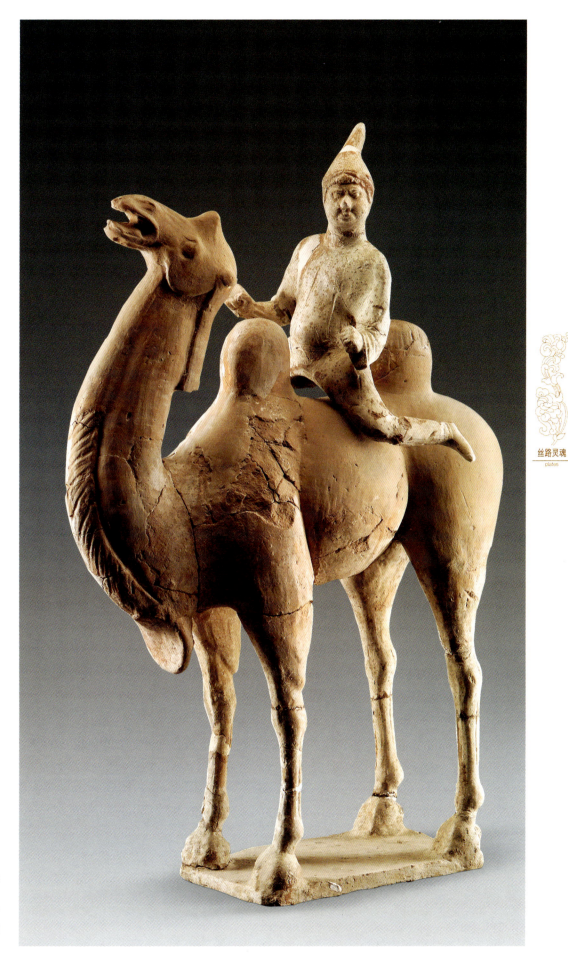

唐陶彩绘胡人骑驼俑
高55、宽21、长40厘米
现藏陕西省考古研究院

**Figurine of painted pottery
Hu camel rider**

55cm high, 21cm wide,
40cm long
Housed at Shaanxi Provincial
Academy of Archaeology

唐胡商俑

高23.5厘米
河南洛阳出土

Figurine of Hu merchant

23.5cm high
Unearthed in Luoyang, Henan

唐绿釉胡人俑

高31.7厘米
河南洛阳郊区河南省地
质队家属楼出土

**Figurine of green-glazed
ceramic man**

31.7cm high
Unearthed from beneath the
building of Henan Geology
Team in the suburb of
Luoyang, Henan

唐黄绿釉执壶男胡俑

高28.5厘米
河南洛阳出土

**Figurine of yellow-green-
glazed ceramic Hu man
holding a vessel**

28.5cm high
Unearthed in Luoyang,
Henan

唐黄釉男胡俑

高30厘米
1972年河南洛阳矿山厂出土

**Figurine of yellow-glazed
ceramic Hu man**

30cm high
Unearthed in Kuangshanchang,
Luoyang, Henan, 1972

唐三彩胡人俑

高66厘米
1963年河南洛阳郊区关林出土

**Figurine of three-color glazed
ceramic Hu man**

66cm high
Unearthed in Guanlin, suburb of
Luoyang, Henan, 1963

唐黄釉胡人俑

高14厘米
1976年河南洛阳矿山厂出土

Figurine of yellow-glazed ceramic Hu man

14cm high
Unearthed in Kuangshanchang, Luoyang, Henan, 1976

丝路灵魂
plates

71

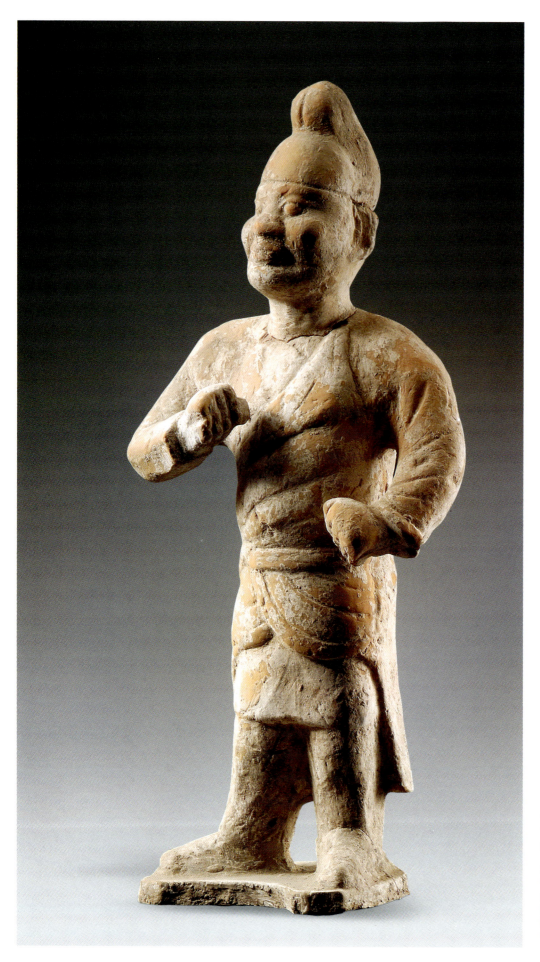

唐陶幞头胡人俑

高34、宽14、厚9厘米
现藏陕西省考古研究院

Figurine of pottery Hu man wearing a head dress

34cm high, 14cm wide, 9cm thick
Housed at Shaanxi Provincial Academy of Archaeology

唐陶幞头胡人俑

高30、宽11、厚8厘米

现藏陕西省考古研究院

**Figurine of pottery Hu
man wearing a head dress**

30cm high, 11cm wide, 8cm
thick
Housed at Shaanxi Provincial
Academy of Archaeology

唐陶幞头胡人俑

高33、宽14.5、厚8.5厘米
现藏陕西省考古研究院

Figurine of pottery Hu man wearing a head dress

33cm high, 14.5cm wide, 8.5cm thick
Housed at Shaanxi Provincial Academy of Archaeology

唐三彩胡人俑

高62.5、宽25、厚19厘米
1972年陕西省乾县唐章
怀太子墓出土
现藏陕西乾陵博物馆

Figurine of three-color glazed ceramic Hu man

62.5cm high, 25cm wide, 19cm thick
Excavated from the tomb of Crown Prince Zhanghuai of Tang dynasty in Qian County, Shaanxi, 1972
Housed at Qianling Museum of Shaanxi

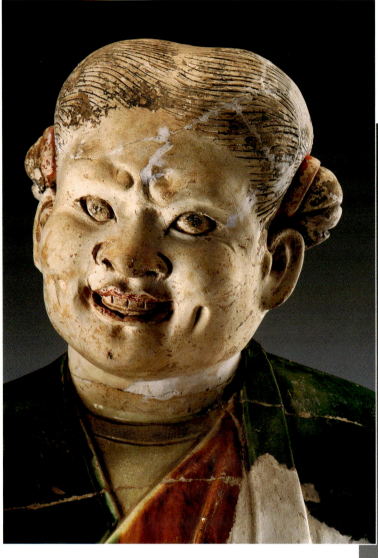

唐三彩胡人俑

高67、宽23、厚19厘米
1972年陕西省乾县唐章怀太子墓出土
现藏陕西乾陵博物馆

Figurine of three-color glazed ceramic Hu person

67cm high, 23cm wide, 19cm thick
Excavated from the tomb of Crown Prince Zhanghuai of Tang
dynasty in Qian County, Shaanxi, 1972
Housed at Qianling Museum of Shaanxi

唐陶幞头胡人俑

高31.5、宽12.5、厚8厘米
现藏陕西省考古研究院

Figurine of pottery Hu man wearing a head dress

31.5cm high, 12.5cm wide, 8cm thick
Housed at Shaanxi Provincial Academy of
Archaeology

唐陶彩绘胡人俑
高55、宽25、厚16厘米
陕西省蒲城县唐惠陵出土
现藏渭南蒲城县博物馆

**Figurine of painted pottery
Hu man**

55cm high, 25cm wide, 16cm
thick
Excavated from the tomb of
Hui Tomb of Tang dynasty in
Pucheng County, Shaanxi
Housed at Pucheng Museum
of Weinan

丝路灵魂
plates

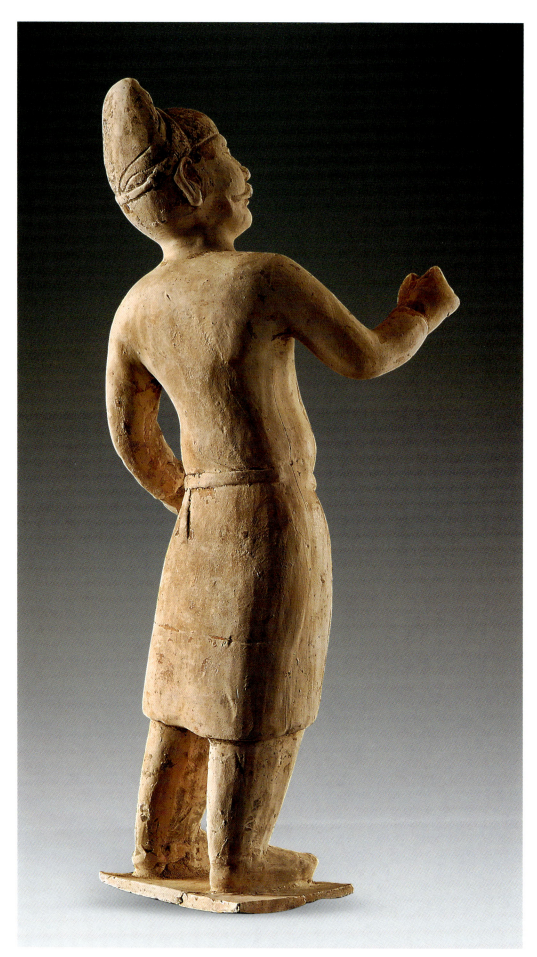

唐陶彩绘胡人俑

高35.5、宽13、厚12厘米
陕西省礼泉县唐张士贵
墓出土
现藏陕西昭陵博物馆

**Figurine of painted
pottery Hu man**

35.5cm high, 13cm wide,
12cm thick
Excavated from the tomb of
Zhang Shigui of Tang dynasty
in Liquan County, Shaanxi
Housed at Zhaoling Museum
of Shaanxi

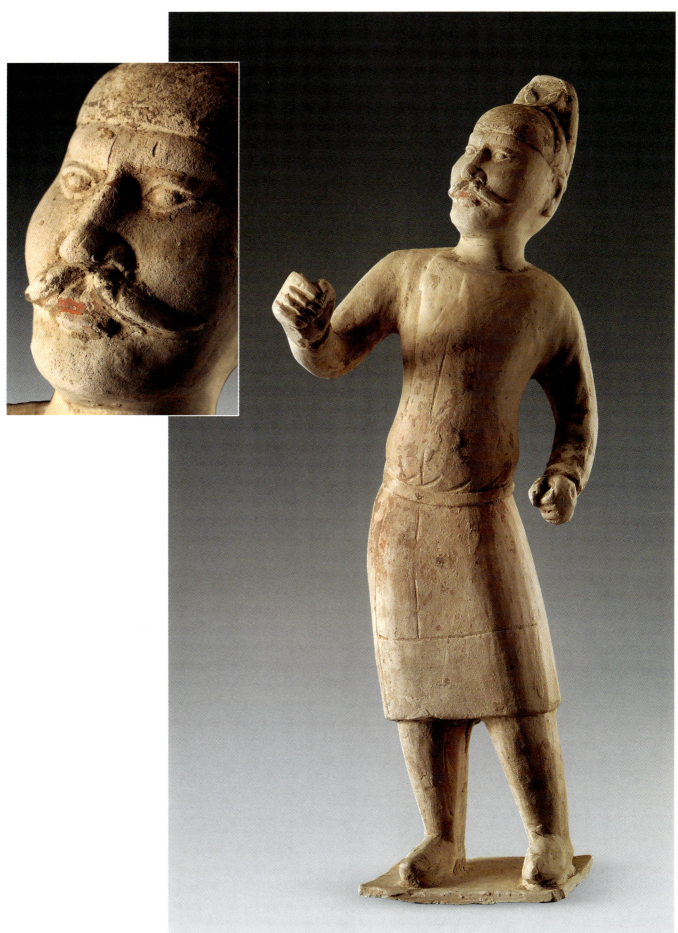

81

唐陶彩绘胡人俑

高29、宽9、厚8厘米
现藏陕西省考古研究院

Figurine of painted pottery Hu man

29cm high, 9cm wide, 8cm thick
Housed at Shaanxi Provincial Academy of Archaeology

丝路灵魂
plates

唐陶彩绘胡人俑

高55、宽26、厚15厘米
陕西省蒲城县唐惠陵出土
现藏渭南市蒲城县博物馆

Figurine of painted pottery Hu man

55cm high, 26cm wide, 15cm thick
Excavated from the tomb of Hui Tomb of
Tang dynasty in Pucheng County, Shaanxi
Housed at Pucheng Museum of Weinan

唐陶幞头胡人俑

高23、宽7、厚5厘米
现藏陕西省考古研究院

Figurine of pottery Hu man wearing a head dress

23cm high, 7cm wide, 5cm thick
Housed at Shaanxi Provincial Academy of Archaeology

唐陶彩绘胡人俑

高55、宽25、厚22厘米
陕西省蒲城县唐惠陵出土
现藏渭南蒲城县博物馆

Figurine of painted pottery Hu man

55cm high, 25cm wide, 22cm thick
Excavated from the tomb of Hui Tomb of Tang dynasty in
Pucheng County, Shaanxi
Housed at Pucheng Museum of Weinan

唐陶彩绘浑脱帽胡人俑

高33、宽16、厚11厘米
现藏陕西省考古研究院

Figurine of painted pottery Hu man wearing a huntuo hat

33cm high, 16cm wide, 11cm thick
Housed at Shaanxi Provincial Academy
Archaeology

唐陶彩绘胡人俑

高64、宽23、厚22厘米
1972年陕西省乾县唐章
怀太子墓出土
现藏陕西乾陵博物馆

**Figurine of painted pottery
Hu man**

64cm high, 23cm wide,
22cm long
Excavated from the tomb
of Princess Yongtai of Tang
dynasty in Qian County,
Shaanxi, 1960
Housed at Qianling Museum
of Shaanxi

唐三彩胡人俑

高53、宽18、厚13厘米
陕西省礼泉县唐李贞墓
出土
现藏陕西昭陵博物馆

**Figurine of three-color
glazed ceramic Hu man**

53cm high, 18cm wide,
13cm thick
Excavated from the tomb of
Li Zhen of Tang dynasty in
Liquan County, Shaanxi
Housed at Zhaoling Museum
of Shanxi

唐陶幞头胡人俑

高23、宽7、厚5厘米
现藏陕西省考古研究院

Figurine of pottery Hu man wearing a head dress

23cm high, 7cm wide, 5cm thick
Housed at Shaanxi Provincial Academy of Archaeology

唐三彩胡人俑

高14、宽6、厚5厘米
陕西省凤翔县箱板纸厂出土
现藏宝鸡凤翔县博物馆

Figurine of three-color glazed ceramic Hu man

14cm high, 6cm wide, 5cm thick
Unearthed in the Fengxiang Cardboard Plant, Shaanxi
Housed at Fengxiang Museum of Baoji

唐陶彩绘胡人俑（左图）

高69、宽23、厚21厘米
1972年陕西省乾县唐章怀太子墓出土
现藏陕西乾陵博物馆

Figurine of painted pottery Hu man

69cm high, 23cm wide, 21cm thick
Excavated from the tomb of Princess Yongtai of Tang dynasty
in Qian County, Shaanxi, 1960
Housed at Qianling Museum of Shaanxi

丝路灵魂
plates

唐三彩胡人俑

高47.5、宽17、厚13厘米
1984年西安市西郊胶合板厂福利区出土
现藏陕西历史博物

Figurine of three-color glazed ceramic Hu man

47.5cm high, 17cm wide, 13cm thick
Unearthed in the living quarter of the Plywood Plant
in the western suburb of Xi'an, 1984
Housed at Shaanxi History Museum

唐三彩胡人俑

高60、宽23、厚19厘米
1972年陕西省乾县唐章怀太子墓出土
现藏陕西乾陵博物馆

Figurine of three-color glazed ceramic Hu man

60cm high, 23cm wide, 19cm thick
Excavated from the tomb of Crown Prince Zhanghuai of Tang dynasty in Qian County, Shaanxi, 1972
Housed at Qianling Museum of Shaanxi

唐陶彩绘胡人俑

高17、宽11、长17厘米
现藏渭南富平县文物旅游局

Figurine of painted pottery Hu man

17cm high, 11cm wide, 17cm long
Housed at the Cultural Relic and Tourism Bureau of Fuping County
of Weinan

丝路灵魂
plates

唐三彩胡人俑

高67.5、宽24、厚18厘米
1972年陕西省乾县唐章
怀太子墓出土
现藏陕西乾陵博物馆

**Figurine of three-color
glazed ceramic Hu man**

67.5cm high, 24cm wide,
18cm thick
Excavated from the tomb
of Crown Prince Zhanghuai
of Tang dynasty in Qian
County, Shaanxi, 1972
Housed at Qianling Museum
of Shaanxi

唐三彩胡人俑

高53、宽16、厚15.5厘米
1972年陕西省乾县唐章
怀太子墓出土
现藏陕西乾陵博物馆

**Figurine of three-color
glazed ceramic Hu man**

53cm high, 16cm wide,
15.5cm thick
Excavated from the tomb
of Crown Prince Zhanghuai
of Tang dynasty in Qian
County, Shaanxi, 1972
Housed at Qianling Museum
of Shaanxi

唐陶幞头胡人俑

高33、宽11.5、厚8厘米
现藏陕西省考古研究院

**Figurine of pottery Hu
man wearing a head dress**

33cm high, 11.5cm wide,
8cm thick
Housed at Shaanxi Provincial
Academy of Archaeology

唐三彩胡人俑

高46厘米
1971年洛阳郊区关林车
圪垱出土

**Figurine of three-color
glazed ceramic Hu man**

46cm high
Unearthed in Chegedang,
suburb of Luoyang, Henan,
1971

唐绿釉胡俑

高31.3厘米
河南洛阳出土

**Figurine of green-glazed
Hu man**

31.3cm high
Unearthed in Luoyang,Henan

唐三彩束发胡人俑

高62厘米
1981年河南洛阳龙门东
山安菩墓出土

**Figurine of three-color
glazed ceramic Hu man
with bound hair**

62cm high
Excavated from the tomb
of Anpu in the eastern
mountain of Longmen,
Luoyang, Henan, 1981

唐三彩高胡帽胡人俑

高67.5厘米
1981年河南洛阳龙门东山
安菩墓出土

**Figurine of three-color
glazed ceramic man with
Hu-style high hat**

67.5cm high
Excavated from the tomb of
Anpu in the eastern mountain
of Longmen, Luoyang, Henan,
1981

唐陶胡人俑

高53厘米
2001年甘肃省庆城县出土
现藏甘肃省博物馆

Figurine of pottery Hu man

53cm high
Unearthed in Qingcheng,Gansu,2001
Housed at Gansu Provincial Museum

丝路灵魂

plates

103

唐陶胡人俑

高50厘米
2001年甘肃省庆城县出土
现藏甘肃省博物馆

Figurine of pottery Hu man

50cm high
Unearthed in Qingcheng,
Gansu,2001
Housed at Gansu Provincial
Museum

唐陶胡人俑（右图）

高54厘米
2001年甘肃省庆城县出土
现藏甘肃省博物馆

Figurine of pottery Hu man

54cm high
Unearthed in Qingcheng,
Gansu,2001
Housed at Gansu Provincial
Museum

105

唐陶胡人俑

高50厘米
2001年甘肃省庆城县出土
现藏甘肃省博物馆

**Figurine of pottery Hu
man**

50cm high
Unearthed in Qingcheng,
Gansu,2001
Housed at Gansu Provincial
Museum

唐陶文吏俑

高59厘米
2001年甘肃省庆城县出土

**Figurine of pottery Hu
man**

59 cm high
Unearthed in Qingcheng,
Gansu,2001

唐陶胡人俑

高45厘米
2001年甘肃省庆城县出土

Figurine of pottery Hu man

45 cm high
Unearthed in Qingcheng,
Gansu,2001

唐陶胡人俑

高53厘米
2001年甘肃省庆城县出土

Figurine of pottery Hu man

53cm high
Unearthed in Qingcheng,
Gansu,2001

唐三彩胡人牵马俑、三彩马

俑高72厘米，马高90.5厘米，长92厘米
1965年甘肃省秦安县叶家堡出土
现藏甘肃省博物馆

Figurine of therr-color glazed Hu man leading a house

Figurine:54cm high, house:90.5cm high,92cm long
Unearthed from Yejiapu,Qin'an county,Gansu,1965
Housed at Gansu Provincial mueum

唐骑卧驼胡俑

高43厘米
1960年陕西宝鸡出土

Figurine of Hu man riding a camel

43cm high
Unearthed in Baoji county,Shaanxi,1960

唐陶胡人俑

高87.7厘米
1954年山西长治市王琛墓出土

Figurine of pottery Hu man

87.7cm high
Unearthed from the tomb of Wangchen in Changzhi,
Shan'xi,1954

唐骑马狩猎俑（右图）

高9厘米
1991年陕西省西安东郊唐金乡县主墓出土

Figurine of pottery Hu man riding a house

9cm high
Unearthed from the tomb of Princess Jinxiang in eastern surburb of Xi'an,Shaanxi,1991

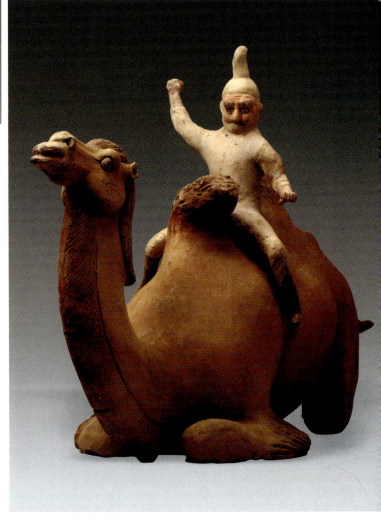

唐胡人骑驼俑

高63厘米
1991年陕西省西安东郊唐金乡县主墓出土

Figurine of Hu man riding a camel

63cm high
Unearthed from the tomb of Princess Jinxiang in eastrern surburb of Xi'an,Shaanxi,1991

唐胡人骑卧驼陶俑

高41厘米
1991年陕西省西安东郊唐金乡县主墓出土

Figurine of pottery Hu man riding a camel

41cm high
Unearthed from the tomb of Princess Jinxiang in eastern surburd of Xi'an, Shaanxi,1991

唐骑马狩猎俑

高35.5、长33.5厘米
1991年陕西省西安东郊唐金乡县主墓
出土

Figurine of Hu man riding a house

35.5cm high,33.5cm long
Unearthed from the tomb of Princess
Jinxiang in eastern suburb of Xi'an,
Shaanxi,1991

唐胡人表演俑

高40.5厘米
1991年陕西省西安东郊唐金乡县主墓出土

Figurine of Hu man

40.5cm high
Unearthed from the tomb of Princess Jinxiang in eastern
surburb of Xi'an, Shaanxi,1991

乐居长安

生活在国际大都会里的胡人
Living in Chang'an: Immigrants in the Metropolis

汉代长安就已经常住许多西域胡人。盛唐时期长安城常住人口多达近百万,是当时世界上最繁华的国际化大都市,居住着大量文化、人种背景迥异的域外来客。《唐六典》载,唐王朝初期曾与300多个国家和地区相互交往,每年都有大批外国使者、僧人及商人通过海陆途径汇集两京,从事政治、商贸和宗教及文化艺术活动。唐都设有鸿胪寺、礼宾院等机构专事接待工作。突厥、波斯、回鹘、契丹、渤海和粟特昭武九姓是客居长安的主要胡人。仅贞观四年随颉利可汗入居长安的突厥人就近万家,占都城人数的近百分之三。有唐一代,胡人客居都城的人数保持在10万人以上,占都城总人口的十分之一以上。

唐陶彩绘胡人俑

高28.5、宽8.5～9、厚6厘米
1987年陕西省陇县东南党家庄村出土
现藏宝鸡陇县博物馆

Figurine of painted pottery Hu man

28.5cm high, 8.5-9cm wide, 6cm thick
Unearthed in Dangjia Zhuang Village, southeast of Long County, Shanxi, 1987
Housed at Long County Museum of Baoji

唐陶彩绘胡人俑

高28、宽9、厚6厘米
1987年陕西省陇县东南党
家庄村出土
现藏宝鸡陇县博物馆

**Figurine of painted pottery
Hu man**

28cm high, 9cm wide, 6cm
thick
Unearthed in Dangjiazhuang
Village, southeast of Long
county, Shaanxi, 1987
Housed at Long County
Museum of Baoji

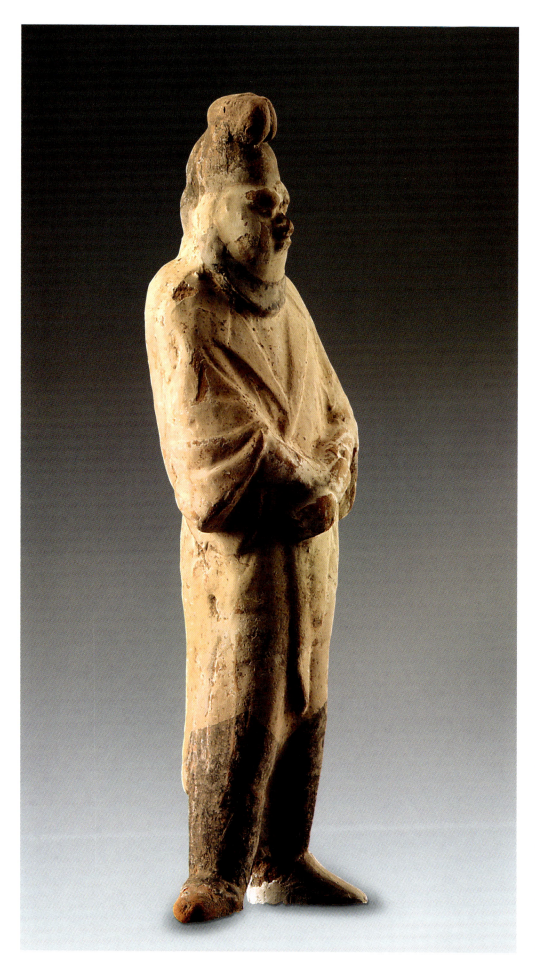

唐陶彩绘胡人俑

高28、宽9、厚6厘米
1987年陕西省陇县东南党
家庄村出土
现藏宝鸡陇县博物馆

**Figurine of painted pottery
Hu man**

28cm high, 9cm wide, 6cm
thick
Unearthed in Dangjiazhuang
Village, southeast of Long
county, Shaanxi, 1987
Housed at Long County
Museum of Baoji

唐陶彩绘胡人俑

高22、宽6、厚5厘米
2003年陕西省陇县城关镇店子村出土
现藏宝鸡陇县博物馆

Figure of painted pottery Hu man

22cm high, 6cm wide, 5cm thick
Unearthed in Dianzi Village, Chengguan
Town, Long County, Shaanxi, 2003
Housed at Long County Museum of Baoji

唐陶彩绘胡人俑

高22、宽6、厚5厘米
2003年陕西省陇县城关镇店子村出土
现藏宝鸡陇县博物馆

Figure of painted pottery Hu man

22cm high, 6cm wide, 5cm thick
Unearthed in Dianzi Village, Chengguan Town, Long County,
Shaanxi, 2003
Housed at Long County Museum of Baoji

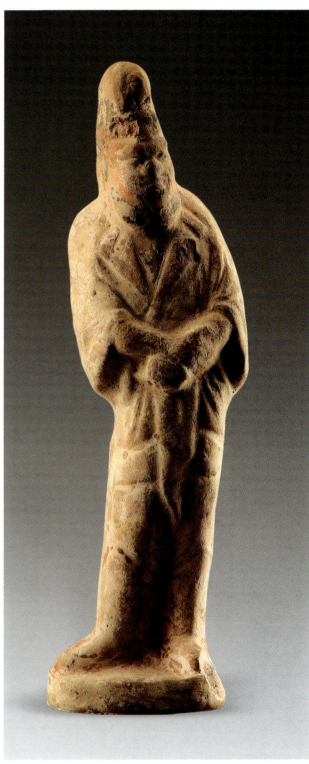

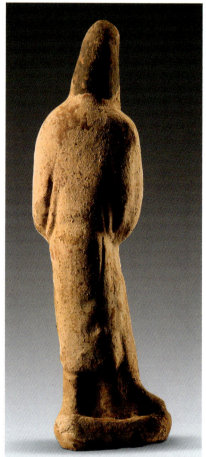

唐陶彩绘胡人俑

高28.5、宽9、厚6厘米
陕西省陇县出土
现藏宝鸡陇县博物馆

Figurine of painted pottery Hu man

28.5cm high, 9cm wide, 6cm thick
Unearthed in Long County, Shaanxi
Housed at Long County Museum of Baoji

乐居长安

plates

唐陶彩绘胡人俑

高21.5、宽6.5、厚4.5厘米
1957年陕西省陇县城关镇祁家庄村出土
现藏宝鸡陇县博物馆

Figurine of painted pottery Hu man

21.5cm high, 6.5cm wide, 4.5cm thick
Unearthed in Qijiazhuang Village, Chengguan Town, Long
County, Shaanxi, 1957
Housed at Long County Museum of Baoji

123

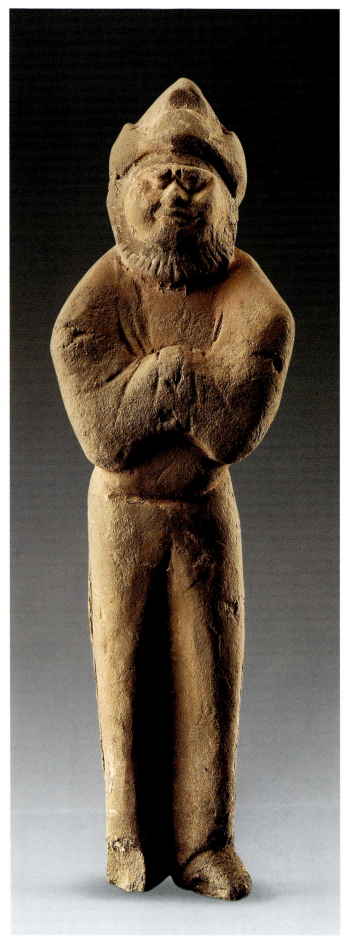

唐陶彩绘胡人俑

高22、宽6.5、厚5厘米
1958年陕西省陇县城关镇北坡村出土
现藏宝鸡陇县博物馆

Figurine of painted pottery Hu man

22cm high, 6.5cm wide, 5cm thick
Unearthed in Beipo Village, Chengguan
Town, Long County, Shaanxi, 1958
House at Long County Museum of Baoji

唐陶彩绘胡人俑

高21.5、宽6.5、厚4.5厘米
1984年陕西省陇县城关镇晁家坡村出土
现藏宝鸡陇县博物馆

Figurine of painted pottery Hu man

21.5cm high, 6.5cm wide, 4.5cm thick
Unearthed in Chaojiapo Village, Chengguan Town, Long
County, Shaanxi, 1984
Housed at Long County Museum of Baoji

唐陶彩绘胡人俑
高27、宽8、厚6厘米
西安市郊区出土
现藏陕西历史博物馆

Figurine of painted pottery Hu man

27cm high, 8cm wide, 6cm thick
Unearthed in the suburb of Xi'an
Housed at Shaanxi History Museum

乐居长安

plates

唐三彩胡人俑

高28、宽11、厚7厘米
1955年陕西省西安东郊韩森寨出土
现藏陕西历史博物馆

Figurine of three-color glazed ceramic Hu man

28cm high, 11cm wide, 7cm thick
Unearthed in Hansenzhai in eastern suburb of Xi'an, 1955
Housed at Shaanxi History Museum

唐陶双垂髻女胡人俑

高30.5、宽11、厚6.5厘米
现藏陕西省考古研究院

**Figurine of pottery Hu
woman with double bun
hairstyle**

30.5cm high, 11cm wide,
6.5cm thick
Housed at Shaanxi Provincial
Academy of Archaeology

唐陶彩绘胡人俑

高31、宽15、厚9.5厘米
现藏陕西省考古研究院

Figurine of painted pottery Hu man

31cm high, 15cm wide, 9.5cm thick
Housed at Shaanxi Provincial Academy of Archaeology

唐陶彩绘幞头胡人俑

高30.5、宽10.5、厚6厘米
现藏陕西省考古研究院

Figurine of painted pottery Hu man wearing a head dress

30.5cm high, 10.5cm wide, 6cm thick
Housed at Shaanxi Provincial Academy of Archaeology

唐陶彩绘幞头胡人俑

高31、宽10.5、厚6.5厘米

现藏陕西省考古研究院

**Figurine of painted pottery Hu man
wearing a head dress**

31cm high, 10.5cm wide, 6.5cm thick
Housed at Shaanxi Provincial Academy of
Archaeology

唐陶彩绘盘发男装女胡人俑

高31、宽16、厚9厘米
现藏陕西省考古研究院

Figurine of painted pottery Hu woman with hair-up style in man's suit

31cm high, 16cm wide, 9cm thick
Housed at Shaanxi Provincial Academy of Archaeology

唐陶彩绘双垂髻男装女胡人俑

高30、宽9.5、厚7.5厘米
现藏陕西省考古研究院

Figurine of painted pottery Hu woman with double bun hairstyle in man's suit

30cm high, 9.5cm wide, 7.5cm thick
Housed at Shaanxi Provincial Academy of Archaeology

唐陶彩绘胡人俑

高19.5、宽7、厚6厘米
陕西省西安市郊区出土
现藏陕西历史博物馆

Figurine of painted pottery Hu man

19.5cm high, 7cm wide, 6cm thick
Unearthed in the suburb of Xi'an
Housed at Shaanxi History Museum

135

唐陶彩绘胡人俑

高35、宽14、厚8.5厘米
1988年西安铁路公安局审
查组交
现藏陕西历史博物馆

**Figurine of painted pottery
Hu man**

35cm high,14cm wide, 8.5cm
thick
Submitted by the Investigation
Group of Xi'an Railway Public
Security Bureau in 1988
Housed at Shaanxi History
Museum

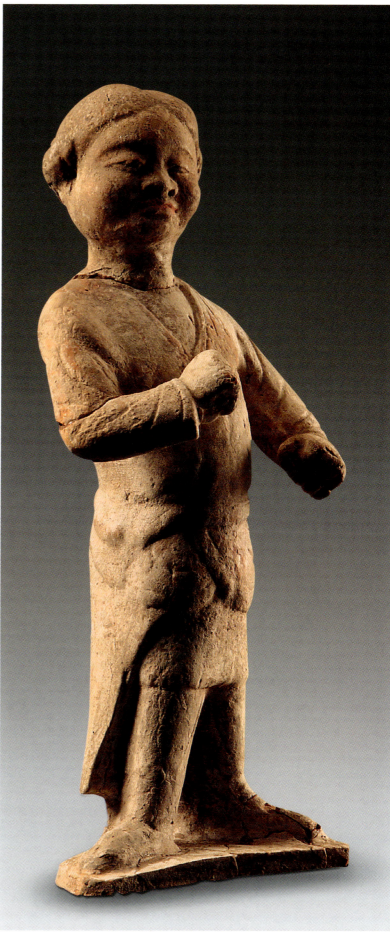

唐陶彩绘盘发男装女胡人俑

高31、宽15、厚9.5厘米

现藏陕西省考古研究院

Figurine of painted pottery Hu woman with hair-up style in man's suit

31cm high, 15cm wide, 9.5cm thick

Housed at Shaanxi Provincial Academy of Archaeology

唐陶彩绘浑脱帽胡人俑

高31.5、宽13、厚10.5
厘米
现藏陕西省考古研究院

**Figurine of painted pottery
Hu man wearing huntuo
hat**

31.5cm high, 13cm wide,
10.5cm thick
Housed at Shaanxi Provincial
Academy of Archaeology

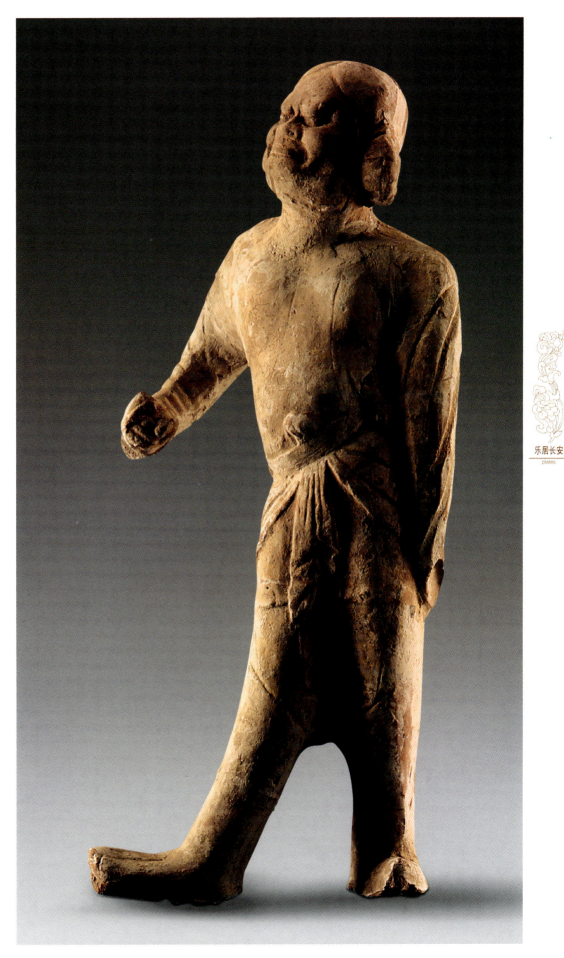

唐陶彩绘胡人俑
高36.5、宽16、厚8.5厘米
1954年陕西省西安市灞
桥出土
现藏陕西历史博物馆

**Figurine of painted pottery
Hu man**

36.5cm high, 16cm wide,
8.5cm thick
Unearthed in Baqiao, Xi'an,
Shaanxi, 1954
Housed at Shaanxi History
Museum

乐居长安
plates

唐陶彩绘胡人俑

高35.5、宽9.5、厚7.5
厘米
1956年陕西省西安市韩
森寨出土
现藏陕西历史博物馆

**Figurine of painted pottery
Hu man**

35.5cm high, 9.5cm wide,
7.5cm thick
Unearthed in Hansenzhai,
Xi'an, 1956
Housed at Shaanxi History
Museum

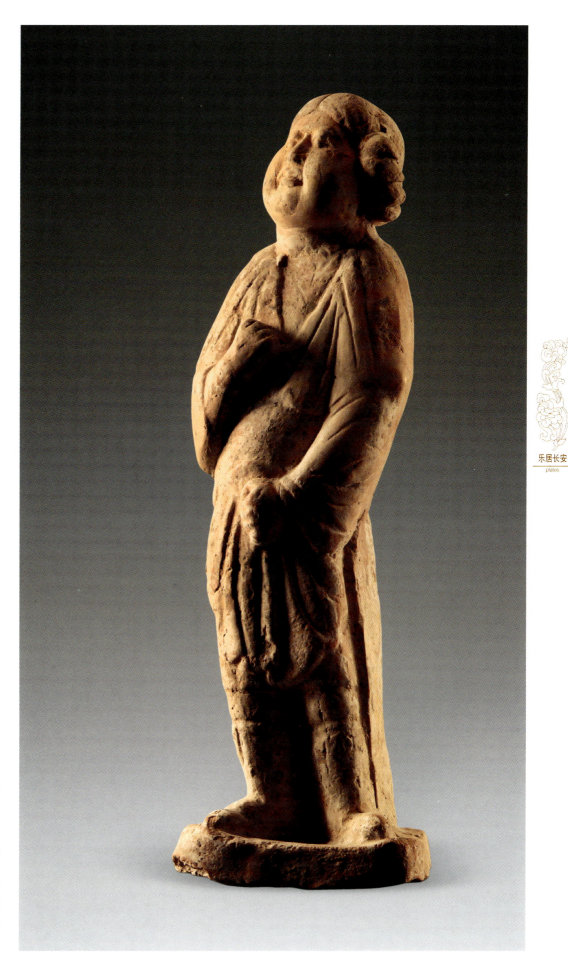

唐陶彩绘胡人俑
高31.5、宽9.5、厚8厘米
陕西省西安市陕棉十厂
出土
现藏陕西省考古研究院

Figurine of painted pottery Hu man

31.5cm high, 9.5cm wide, 8cm thick
Unearthed in Shaanxi Tenth Cotton Plant of Xi'an
Housed at Shaanxi Provincial Academy of Archaeology

唐陶彩绘双垂髻男装女胡人俑

高30、宽10、厚6.5厘米
现藏陕西省考古研究院

Figurine of painted pottery Hu woman with double bun hairstyle in man's suit

30cm high, 10cm wide, 6.5cm thick
Housed at Shaanxi Provincial Academy of Archaeology

唐陶彩绘胡人俑

高46.5、宽18.5、厚11
厘米
陕西省咸阳市底张湾出土
现藏陕西历史博物馆

**Figurine of painted pottery
Hu man**

46.5cm high, 18.5cm wide,
11cm thick
Unearthed in Dizhangwan,
Xianyang, Shaanxi
Housed at Shaanxi History
Museum

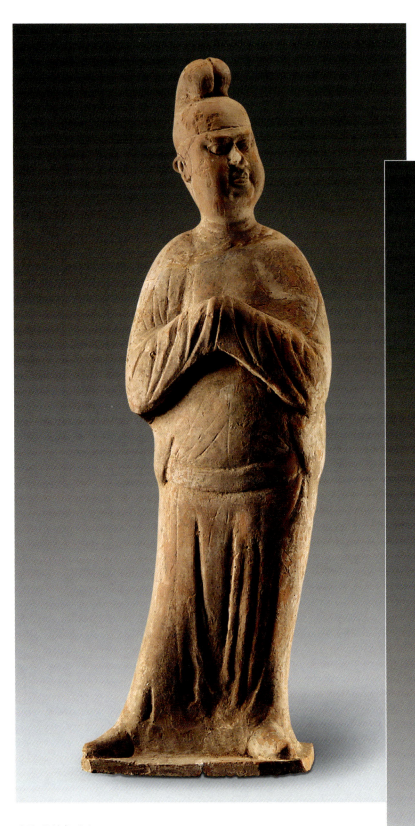

唐陶彩绘胡人俑

高62、宽23、厚18厘米
陕西省西安市出土
现藏陕西历史博物馆

Figurine of painted pottery Hu man

62cm high, 23cm wide, 18cm thick
Unearthed in Xi'an, Shaanxi
Housed at Shaanxi History Museum

唐陶彩绘武士俑

高49、宽17、厚15厘米
陕西省礼泉县唐王君愕墓出土
现藏陕西昭陵博物馆

Figurine of painted pottery solider

49cm high, 17cm wide, 15cm thick
Excavated from the tomb of Wang Jun'e of Tang dynasty in
Liquan County, Shaanxi
Housed at Zhaoling Museum of Shaanxi

唐陶彩绘胡人俑

高24、宽7.5、厚6厘米
陕西省礼泉县唐张士贵墓出土
现藏陕西昭陵博物馆

Figurine of painted pottery Hu man

24cm high, 7.5cm wide, 6cm thick
Excavated from the tomb of Zhang Shigui of Tang
dynasty in Liquan County, Shaanxi
Housed at Zhaoling Museum of Shaanxi

唐三彩袒腹胡人俑

高18厘米
1960年陕西省乾县唐永泰公主墓出土
现存陕西历史博物馆

**Figurine of three-color glazed ceramic Hu man
with bare belly**

18cm high
Excavated from the tomb of Princess Yongtai of Tang
dynasty in Qian County, Shaanxi, 1960
Housed at Shaanxi History Museum

唐彩绘胡人俑

高65.5厘米
2001年陕西长安郭杜镇出土

Figurine of painted Hu man

65.5cm high
Excavated from Guodu,Chang'an ,Shaanxi,2001

唐彩绘胡人文吏俑

高41厘米
1985陕西省三原县出土
现藏陕西历史博物馆

Figurine of painted Hu civilian official

41cm high
Unearthed in Sanyuan County, Shaanxi, 1985
Housed at Shaanxi History Museum

唐三彩胡人俑

高42.6厘米
2002年西安南郊唐墓出土

**Figurine of three-color
glazed ceramic Hu man**

42.6cm high
Unearthed from the tomb
of Tang dynasty in southrn
surburd of xi'an,2002

唐胡人俑头

高15厘米
1955年西安郊区出土
藏陕西历史博物馆

Figurine head of Hu man

15cm high
Unearthed in surburb of Xi'an,Shaanxi,1955
Housed at Shaanxi History Museum

唐胡人俑

高26.8厘米
1955年西安韩森寨出土

Figurine of Hu man

26.8cm high
Unearthed from Hansenzhai of Xi'an,Shaan'xi,1955

151

唐骑驼奏乐胡人俑

高50.1、长40.5厘米
2002年西安南郊唐墓出土

Figurine of Hu man riding a camel

50.1cm high,40.5cm long
Unearthed from the tomb of Tang dynasty in
southern surburd of Xi'an, Shaanxi,2002

唐白瓷胡俑头

高16.5厘米
1965年西安东郊段伯阳墓出土

Figurine head of white porcelain Hu man

16.5cm high
Unearthed from the tomb of Duanboyang in eastern surburb of Xi'an,
Shaanxi,1965

第四单元

胡风东渐

胡人对唐代文明的影响

Eastward Spread of the Exotic Custom: Influences of the Foreigners on the Civilization of Tang China

唐代的空前开放，缘于对本土文化的自信和自豪，整个国家洋溢着一种积极向上的精神状态。对外来精神文化，以"海纳百川"的博大胸怀，为我所用，使华夏文明益显成熟丰满，光彩照人；对外来物质文化的优秀成果在欣然接受后，又加以改进，使之更为先进；对外来人民妥善安置，并与汉人和谐相处，使中国古代的民族融合达到一个新的阶段。

唐陶彩绘胡人骑马俑

高50、宽13、长47厘米
陕西省礼泉县唐韦贵妃墓出土
现藏陕西昭陵博物馆

Figurine of painted pottery Hu horse rider

50cm high, 13cm wide, 47cm long
Excavated from the tomb of Consort Wei of Tang
dynasty in Liquan County, Shaanxi
Housed at Zhaoling Museum of Shaanxi

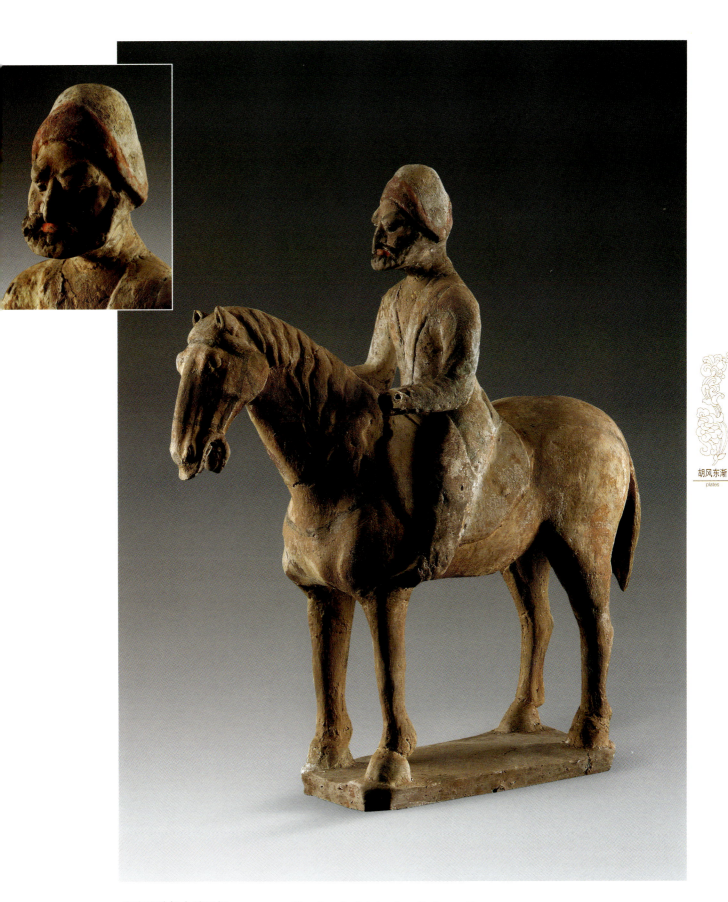

唐陶彩绘胡人骑马俑

高36.5、宽11、长33厘米
陕西省礼泉县唐段简璧墓出土
现藏陕西昭陵博物馆

Figurine of painted pottery Hu horse rider

36.5cm high, 11cm wide, 33cm long
Excavated from the tomb of Duan Jianbi of Tang dynasty in
Liquan County, Shaanxi
Housed at Zhaoling Museum of Shaanxi

胡风东渐
plates

157

唐陶彩绘胡人骑马俑

高30.5、宽9.5、长26.5厘米
1960年陕西省乾县唐永泰公主墓出土
现藏陕西乾陵博物馆

Figurine of painted pottery Hu horse rider

30.5cm high, 9.5cm wide, 26.5cm long
Excavated from the tomb of Princess Yongtai of Tang dynasty
in Qian County, Shaanxi, 1960
Housed at Qianling Museum of Shaanxi

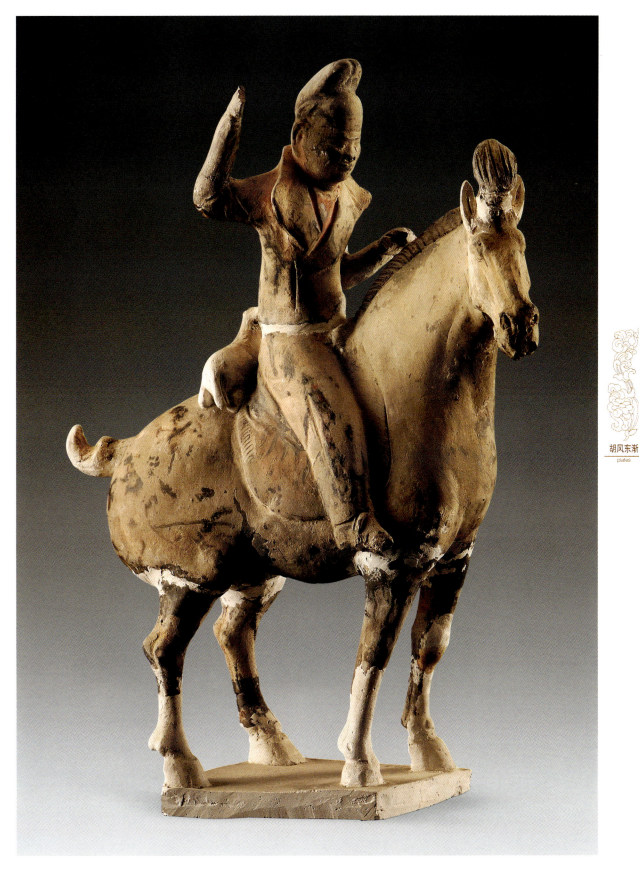

唐陶彩绘骑马狩猎俑

高30.5、宽11、长22厘米
1960年陕西省乾县唐永泰公主墓出土
现藏陕西乾陵博物馆

Figurine of painted pottery riding hunter

30.5cm high, 11cm wide, 22cm long
Excavated from the tomb of Princess Yongtai of Tang dynasty in
Qian County, Shaanxi, 1960
Housed at Qianling Museum of Shaanxi

唐陶彩绘胡人骑马俑

高50、宽14、长45厘米
陕西省礼泉县唐韦贵妃墓出土
现藏陕西昭陵博物馆

Figurine of painted pottery Hu horse rider

50cm high, 14cm wide, 45cm long
Excavated from the tomb of Consort Wei of Tang dynasty in
Liquan County, Shaanxi
Housed at Zhaoling Museum of Shaanxi

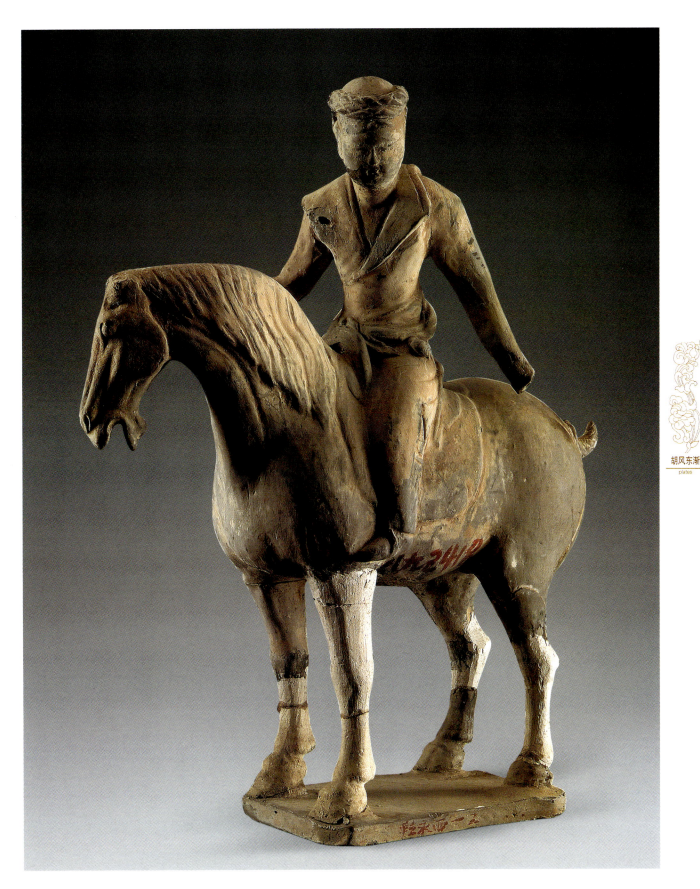

唐陶彩绘胡人骑马俑

高29、宽8、长24厘米
1960年陕西省乾县唐永泰公主墓出土
现藏陕西乾陵博物馆

Figurine of painted pottery Hu horse rider

29cm high, 8cm wide, 24cm long
Excavated from the tomb of Princess Yongtai of Tang dynasty in
Qian County, Shaanxi, 1960
Housed at Qianling Museum of Shaanxi

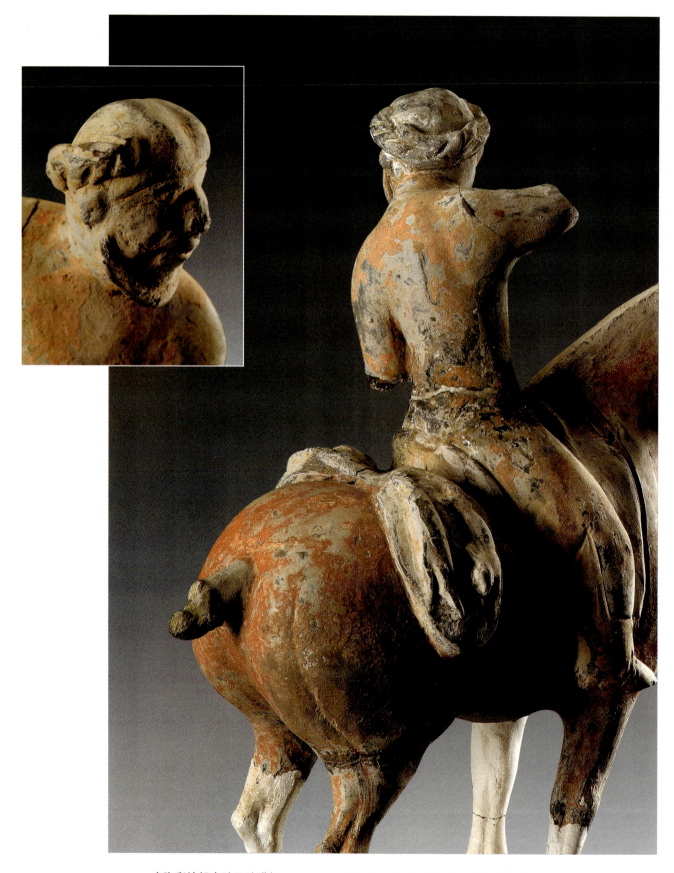

唐陶彩绘胡人骑马狩猎俑

高28、宽9、长24厘米
1960年陕西省乾县唐永泰公主墓出土
现藏陕西乾陵博物馆

Figurine of painted pottery Hu riding hunter

28cm high, 9cm wide, 24cm long
Excavated from the tomb of Princess Yongtai of Tang dynasty
in Qian County, Shaanxi, 1960
Housed at Qianling Museum of Shaanxi

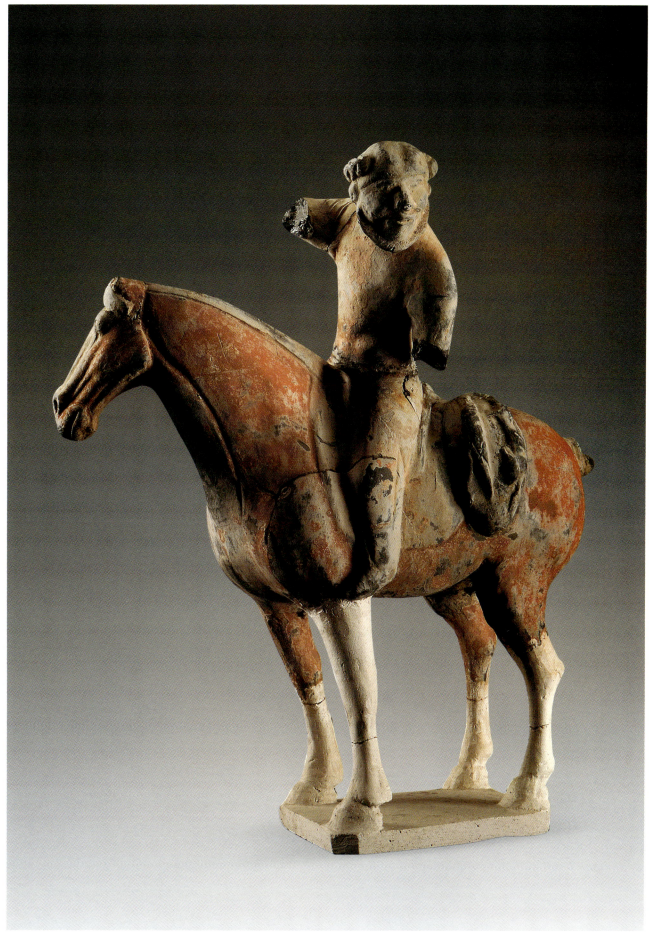

胡风东渐
plates

唐陶彩绘虎头盔甲骑具装俑

高26、宽9、长23厘米

现藏陕西省考古研究院

Figurine of painted pottery horse rider with tiger-style helmet and armor

26cm high, 9cm wide, 23cm long

Housed at Shaanxi Provincial Academy of Archaeology

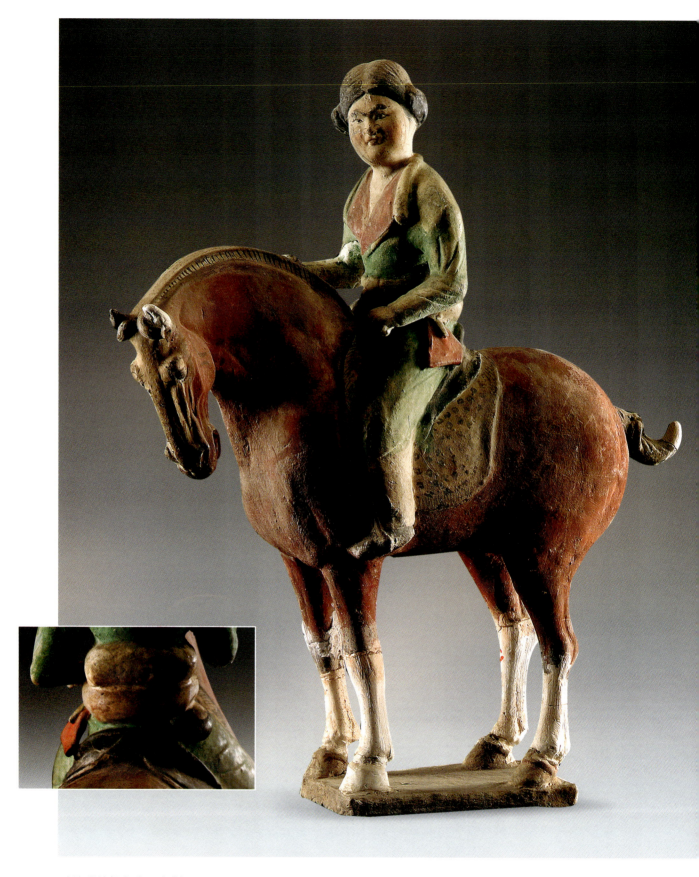

唐陶彩绘胡人骑马狩猎俑

高34、宽11、长28厘米
1960年陕西省乾县唐永泰公主墓出土
现藏陕西乾陵博物馆

Figurine of painted pottery Hu riding hunter

34cm high, 11cm wide, 28cm long
Excavated from the tomb of Princess Yongtai of Tang dynasty
in Qian County, Shaanxi, 1960
Housed at Qianling Museum of Shaanxi

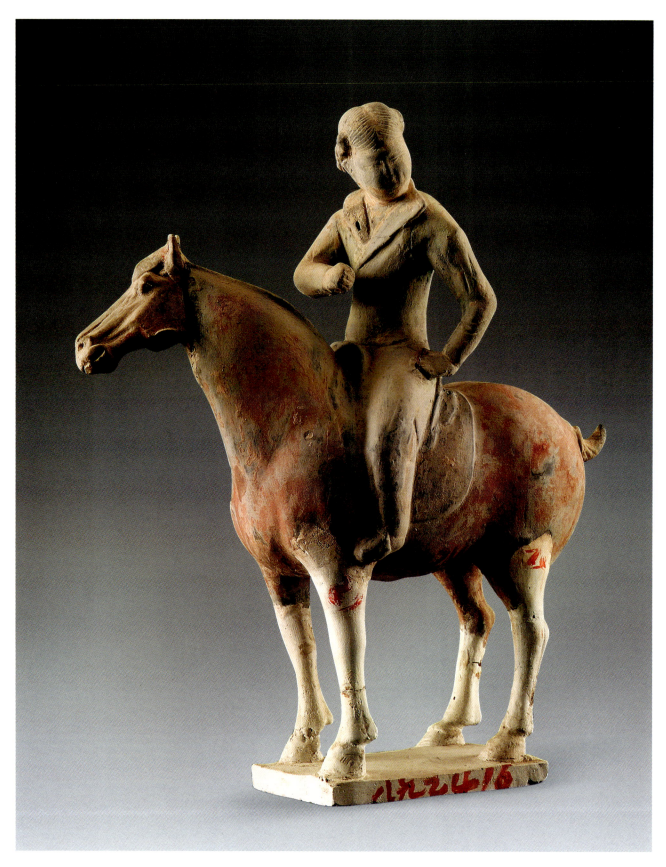

唐陶彩绘胡人骑马俑

高34、宽11、长28厘米
1960年陕西省乾县唐永泰公主墓出土
现藏陕西乾陵博物馆

Figurine of painted pottery Hu horse rider

34cm high, 11cm wide, 28cm long
Excavated from the tomb of Princess Yongtai of Tang dynasty in Qian
County, Shaanxi, 1960
Housed at Qianling Museum of Shaanxi

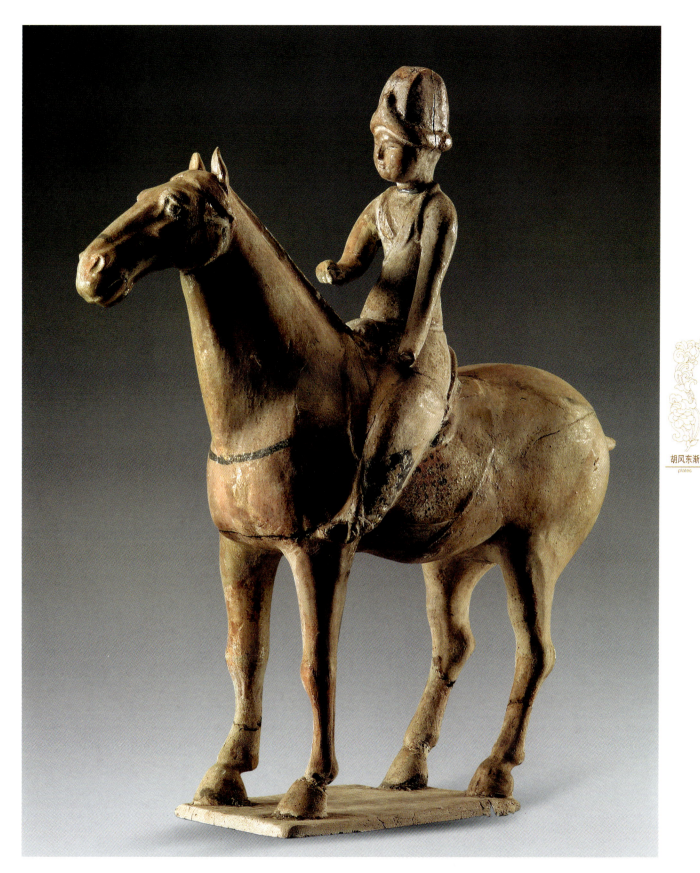

唐彩绘釉陶戴胡帽女骑马俑

高42、宽12、长40厘米
陕西省礼泉县唐郑仁泰墓出土
现藏陕西昭陵博物馆

Figurine of painted glazed pottery woman horse rider with a Hu-style hat

42cm high, 12cm wide, 40cm long
Excavated from the tomb of Zheng Rentai in Liquan County, Shaanxi
Housed at Zhaoling Museum of Shaanxi

169

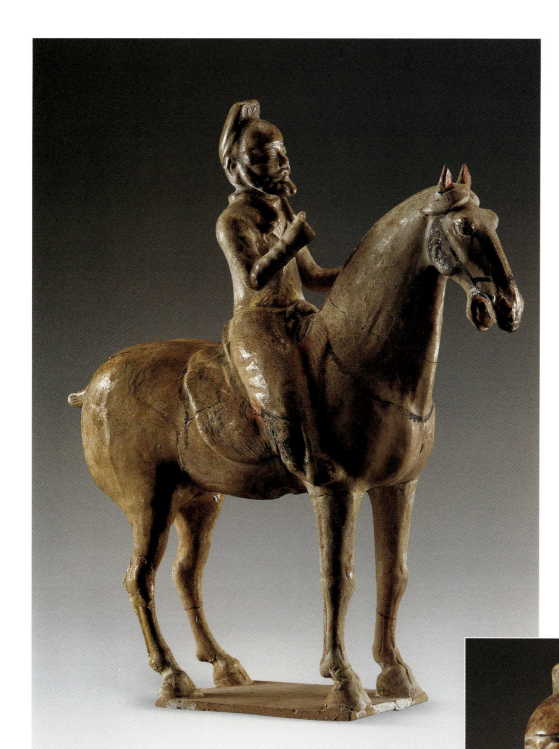

胡风东渐
plates

唐彩绘釉陶骑马俑

高42、宽13、长35厘米
陕西省礼泉县唐郑仁泰墓出土
现藏陕西昭陵博物馆

Figurine of painted glazed pottery horse rider

42cm high, 13cm wide, 35cm long
Excavated from the tomb of Zheng Rentai
in Liquan County, Shaanxi
Housed at Zhaoling Museum of Shaanxi

唐彩绘釉陶骑马俑

高40、宽11、长36厘米
陕西省礼泉县唐郑仁泰墓出土
现藏陕西昭陵博物馆

Figurine of painted glazed pottery horse rider

40cm high, 11cm wide, 36cm long
Excavated from the tomb of Zheng Rentai
in Liquan County, Shaanxi
Housed at Zhaoling Museum of Shaanxi

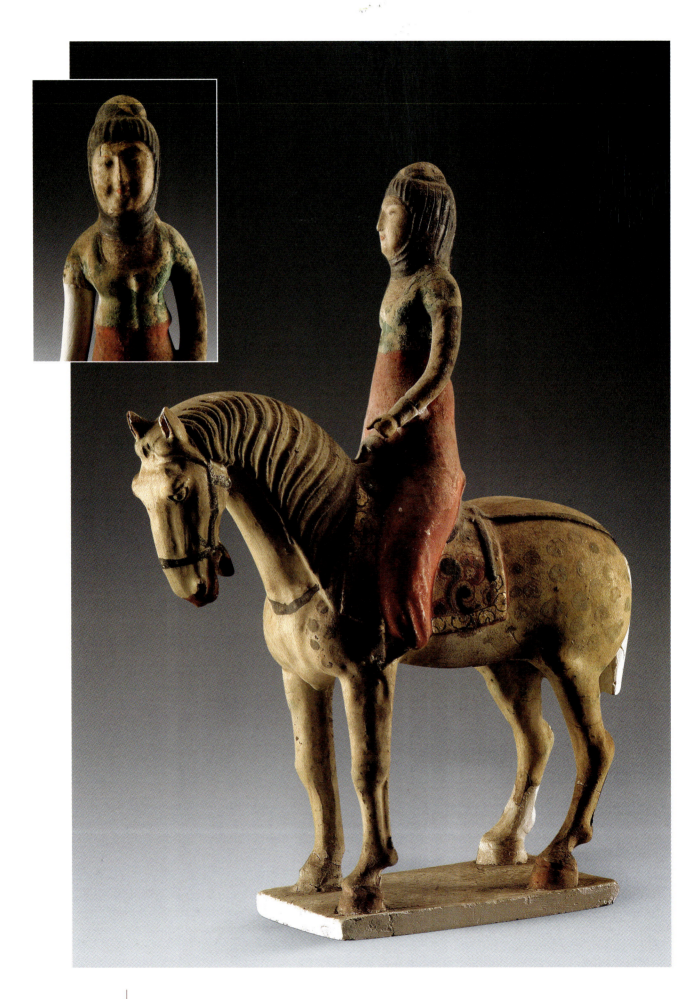

唐白瓷胡人俑

高19、宽5、厚4厘米
陕西省咸阳地区出土
现藏陕西咸阳文物保护中心

Figurine of white porcelain Hu man

19cm high, 5cm wide, 4cm thick
Unearthed in Xianyang, Shaanxi
Housed at Xianyang Cultural Relic Conservation Centre of
Shaanxi

唐彩绘釉陶戴幂篱女骑马俑

高36、宽12、长28厘米
陕西省礼泉县唐郑仁泰墓出土
现藏陕西昭陵博物馆

**Figurine of painted glazed pottery woman horse rider
with a muli hat**

36cm high, 12cm wide, 28cm long
Excavated from the tomb of Zheng Rentai in Liquan County,
Shaanxi
Housed at Zhaoling Museum of Shaanxi

唐陶彩绘胡人立俑

高19、宽5、厚4厘米
1960年陕西省乾县唐永泰公主墓出土
现藏陕西乾陵博物馆

Figurine of painted standing Hu man

19cm high, 5cm wide, 4cm thick
Excavated from the tomb of Princess Yongtai of Tang dynasty in Qian County, Shaanxi, 1960
Housed at Qianling Museum of Shaanxi

胡风东渐
plates

唐三彩胡人俑

高21、宽4.5、厚4.5厘米
1960年陕西省乾县唐永
泰公主墓出土
现藏陕西乾陵博物馆

**Figurine of three-color
glazed ceramic Hu man**

21cm high, 4.5cm wide,
4.5cm thick
Excavated from the tomb
of Princess Yongtai of Tang
dynasty in Qian County,
Shaanxi, 1960
Housed at Qianling Museum
of Shaanxi

唐三彩胡人骑马狩猎俑

高38、宽13、长32厘米
1972年陕西省乾县唐章怀太子墓出土
现藏陕西乾陵博物馆

Figurine of three-color glazed ceramic Hu riding hunter

38cm high, 13cm wide, 32cm long
Excavated from the tomb of Crown Prince Zhanghuai of Tang
dynasty in Qian County, Shaanxi, 1972
Housed at Qianling Museum of Shaanxi

唐三彩胡人骑马狩猎俑

高39、宽12、长32厘米
1972年陕西省乾县唐章怀太子墓出土
现藏陕西乾陵博物馆

**Figurine of three-color glazed ceramic Hu riding
hunter**

39cm high, 12cm wide, 32cm long
Excavated from the tomb of Crown Prince Zhanghuai of Tang
dynasty in Qian County, Shaanxi, 1972
Housed at Qianling Museum of Shaanxi

唐三彩胡人骑马狩猎俑

高39、宽12、长32厘米
1972年陕西省乾县唐章怀太子墓出土
现藏陕西乾陵博物馆

Figurine of three-color glazed ceramic Hu riding hunter

39cm high, 12cm wide, 32cm long
Excavated from the tomb of Crown Prince Zhanghuai of Tang
dynasty in Qian County, Shaanxi, 1972
Housed at Qianling Museum of Shaanxi

唐三彩胡人骑马狩猎俑

高38、宽12、长32厘米
1972年陕西省乾县唐章怀太子墓出土
现藏陕西乾陵博物馆

Figurine of three-color glazed ceramic Hu riding hunter

38cm high, 12cm wide, 32cm long
Excavated from the tomb of Crown Prince Zhanghuai of Tang
dynasty in Qian Cunty, Shaanxi, 1972
Housed at Qianling Museum of Shaanxi

唐三彩骑马胡人俑

高39、长36厘米
1981年河南洛阳龙门东山安菩
墓出土

Figurine of three-color glazed ceramic male Hu horse rider

39cm high, 36cm long
Excavated from the tomb of Anpu in the eastern mountain of Longmen, Luoyang, Henan, 1981

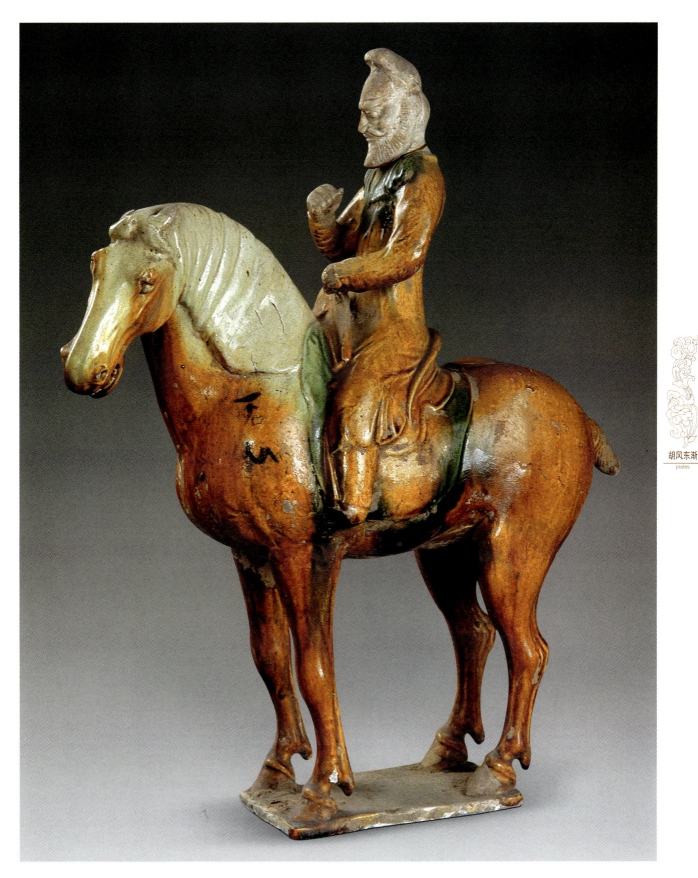

唐三彩骑马胡人俑

高42.2、长36.5厘米
河南洛阳出土

Figurine of three-color glazed ceramic Hu horse rider

42.2cm high, 36.5cm long
Unearthed from Luoyang,Henan

唐三彩胡人骑马狩猎俑

高38、宽13、长32厘米
1972年陕西省乾县唐章怀太子墓出土
现藏陕西乾陵博物馆

Figurine of three-color glazed ceramic Hu riding hunter

38cm high, 13cm wide, 32cm long
Excavated from the tomb of Crown Prince Zhanghuai of Tang
dynasty in Qian County, Shaanxi, 1972
Housed at Qianling Museum of Shaanxi

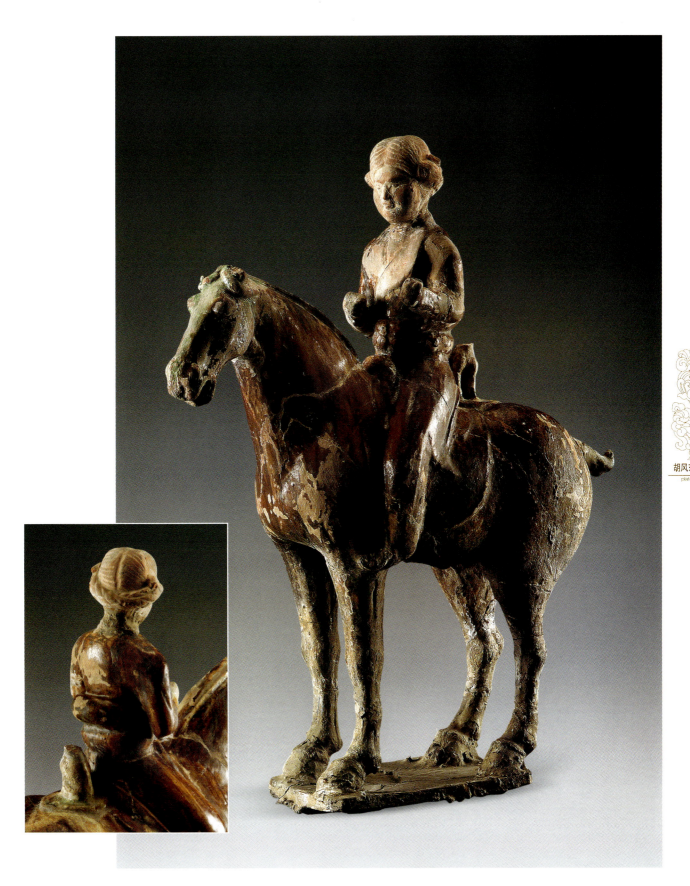

唐三彩胡人骑马狩猎俑

高34、宽13、长32厘米
1972年陕西省乾县唐章怀太子墓出土
现藏陕西乾陵博物馆

Figurine of three-color glazed ceramic Hu riding hunter

34cm high, 13cm wide, 32cm long
Excavated from the tomb of Crown Prince Zhanghuai of Tang
dynasty in Qian County, Shaanxi, 1972
Housed at Qianling Museum of Shaanxi

唐彩绘胡人骑马载物俑

高32、长26厘米
1960年陕西省乾县唐永泰公主墓出土
现存陕西历史博物馆

Figurine of painted Hu man riding on a loaded horse

32cm high, 26cm long
Excavated from the tomb of Princess Yongtai of Tang dynasty
in Qian County, Shaanxi, 1960
Housed at Shaanxi History Museum

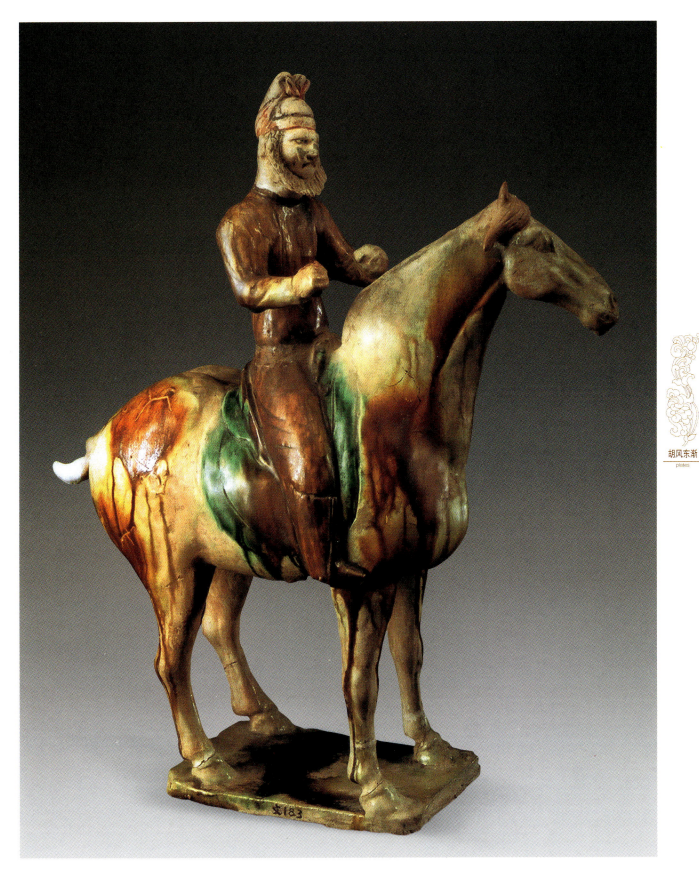

唐三彩胡人骑马俑

高31、长22.5厘米
1971陕西省乾县唐懿德太子墓出土
现存陕西历史博物馆

Figurine of three-color glazed ceramic Hu horse rider

31cm high, 22.5cm long
Excavated from the tomb of Crown Prince Yide of Tang dynasty
in Qian County, Shaanxi, 1971
Housed at Shaanxi History Museum

胡风东渐
plates

唐彩绘说唱俑群

高7～8厘米
1983年陕西省西安市西郊俾失十囊墓出土
现藏陕西历史博物馆

Figurine of painted singers and storytellers

7~8cm high
Excavated from the tomb of Bishishinang in the western suburb of
Xi'an,shaanxi,1983
Housed at Shaanxi History Museum

唐彩绘打马球俑

高35、长30厘米
1959年陕西省西安长安韦泂墓出土

Figurine of painted polo player

35cm high, 30cm long
Excavated from the tomb of Wei Jiong in Chang'an, Xi'an,
Shaanxi, 1959

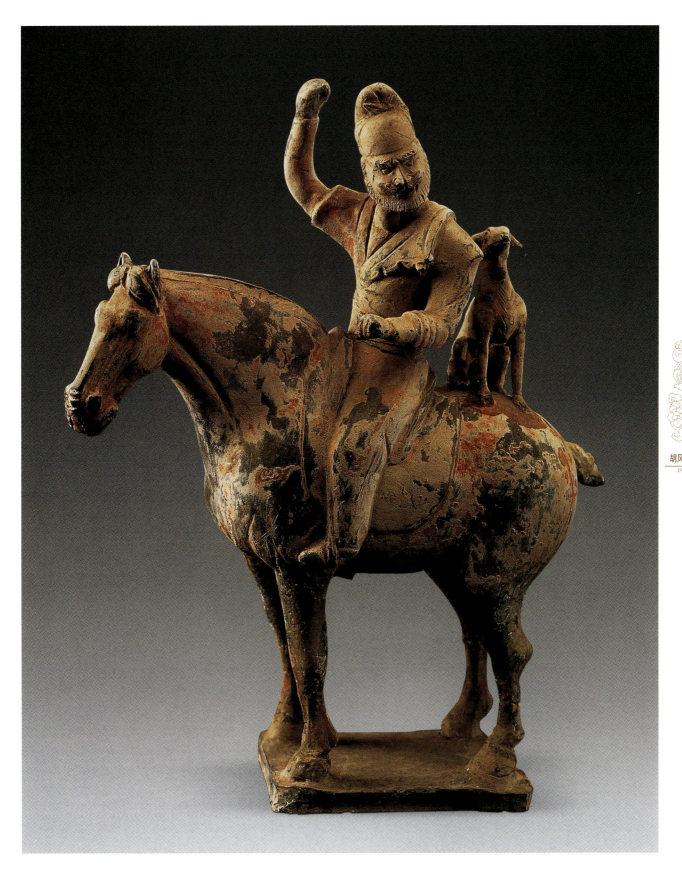

唐彩绘胡人骑马带犬狩猎俑

高31、长33厘米
1960年陕西省乾县唐永泰公主墓出土
现存陕西历史博物馆

Figurine of painted Hu riding hunter, accompanying with a hound

31cm high, 33cm long
Excavated from the tomb of Princess Yongtai of Tang dynasty
in Qian County, Shaanxi, 1960
Housed at Shaanxi History Museum

唐彩绘胡人骑马携豹俑

高30.5厘米
1960年陕西省乾县唐永泰公主墓出土
现存陕西历史博物馆

Figurine of painted Hu horse rider with a leopard

30.5cm high
Excavated from the tomb of Princess Yongtai of Tang dynasty
in Qian County, Shaanxi, 1960
Housed at Shaanxi History Museum

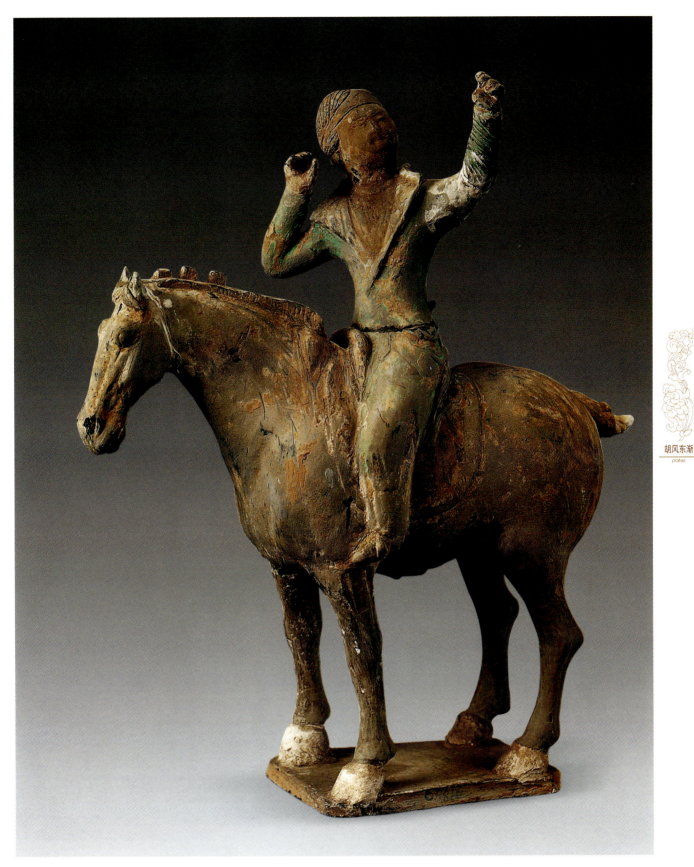

唐彩绘胡人骑马射猎俑

高33、长27厘米
1960年陕西省乾县唐永泰公主墓出土
现存陕西历史博物馆

Figurine of painted Hu riding hunter

33cm high, 22cm long
Excavated from the tomb of Princess Yongtai of Tang dynasty
in Qian County, Shaanxi, 1960
Housed at Shaanxi History Museum

唐彩绘上身裸体骑马胡人俑

高30厘米
1960年陕西省乾县唐永泰公主墓出土
现藏陕西历史博物馆

Figurine of painted Hu man

30cm high
Excavated from the tomb of Princess Yongtai of Tang dynasty
in Qian county,Shaanxi,1960
Housed at Qianling Museum of Shaanxi

附　录

Appendices

隋唐时期胡俑出土统计表

胡俑名称	数量	尺寸	出土时间	出土地点	所属墓葬	时代	资料出处	备注
胡俑	5		1964年11月	陕西三原	李和墓	隋文帝开皇二年（582年）	《陕西省三原县双盛村隋李和墓清理简报》，《文物》1966年第1期	被盗，位置被扰乱；俑身残缺
残俑头	1		1973年7月	安徽合肥		隋文帝开皇六年（586年）	安徽省展览、博物馆《合肥西郊隋墓》，《考古》1976年第2期	被盗，拱顶大部分被破坏
胡俑	2	高25厘米	1959年5月	河南安阳	张盛及其妻王氏墓	隋文帝开皇十五年（595年）	考古研究所安阳发掘队《安阳隋张盛墓发掘记》，《考古》1959年第10期	许多器物没于水中，因此它们的排列位置不清楚
骑骆驼俑	2	高45.5厘米	1980年4月	山西太原	斛律徹墓	隋文帝开皇十七年（597年）	山西省考古研究所、太原市文物管理委员会《太原隋斛律徹墓清理简报》，《文物》1992年第10期	墓室积水，随葬品已不在原来位置
胡人骑马俑	2	高34.5厘米	1984年9月	陕西西安	李椿及其妻刘氏合葬墓	隋炀帝大业三年（607年）	陕西省考古研究所《西安东郊隋李椿夫妇墓清理简报》，《考古与文物》1986年第3期	该墓遭破坏；男骑马俑Ⅰ型
胡俑	2	高32厘米	1973年3月	安徽亳县	隋代□爽墓	同上	亳县博物馆《安徽亳县隋墓》，《考古》1977年第1期	
翻领胡服俑	6		1957年8月	陕西西安	李静训墓	隋炀帝大业四年（608年）	唐金裕《西安西郊隋李静训墓发掘简报》，《考古》1959年第9期	
牵马俑	1		1954年	同上	姬威墓	隋炀帝大业六年（610年）	陕西省文物管理委员会《西安郭家滩隋姬威墓清理简报》，《文物》1959年第8期	被盗，随葬品的位置被扰乱
老人俑	1		同上	同上	同上	同上	同上	同上
陶头俑	不明	一般长8厘米	同上	同上	同上	同上	同上	同上
长胡握物男立俑	1	高22、宽6.5厘米	1975年8月	同上		隋代	王长启《西安发现的汉、隋时期陶俑》，《考古与文物》1992年第2期	该墓并没进行正式发掘
胡俑	9	高22.5厘米	1973年	河南安阳		同上	中国社会科学院考古研究所安阳工作队《安阳隋墓发掘报告》，《考古学报》1981年第3期	没有被盗；分出于三座墓中（103、108、201），每墓出三件
胡俑	1	高16、宽4.2、厚4.2厘米	1981年秋	河南巩义		同上	巩义市博物馆《河南巩义市夹津口隋墓清理简报》，《华夏考古》2005年第4期	该墓破坏严重，随葬品位置已被扰乱
黄绿釉执壶男胡俑		高28.5厘米	1981	河南洛阳		同上	洛阳市文物管理局编《洛阳陶俑》，北京图书出版社2005年	
胡俑	1	高22厘米	1988年5月	湖北武昌		隋代初期	武汉市博物馆《湖北武昌马房山隋墓清理简报》，《考古》1994年第11期	该墓破坏严重；男俑Ⅰ式
胡俑	1	残高13.6厘米	1986年10月	河南安阳		同上	安阳市文物工作队《河南安阳市两座隋墓发掘报告》，《考古》1992年第1期	该墓编号为安阳桥村隋墓；器物位置多没有移动
胡俑	1	高39.7厘米	1982年7月	湖北武汉		隋代大业年间	武汉市文物管理处《武汉市东湖岳家嘴隋墓发掘简报》，《考古》1983年第9期	被盗，大部分器物零散，已非原来的位置
胡俑	5	高23.5厘	1983年3月~1986年10月	河南安阳		隋文帝仁寿年间到隋末	安阳市文物工作队《河南安阳市两座隋墓发掘报告》，《考古》1992年第1期	该墓编号为安阳梅元庄隋墓；被盗
胡人俑	1	高20.8厘米	1998年4月	河北平山	崔仲方墓	唐太宗贞观十一年（637年）	《河北平山县西岳村隋唐崔氏墓》，《考古》2001年第2期	该墓被编号为M2；墓葬被破坏始殆，随葬品原来位置不清
男骑马俑Ⅰ式	4	长22、通高29.5厘米	1986年11月	陕西西安	长乐公主墓	唐太宗贞观十七年（643年）	昭陵博物馆《唐昭陵长乐公主墓》，《文博》1988年第3期	被盗
男骑马俑	2		1984年3月	同上	司马睿墓	唐太宗贞观二十三年（649年）	负安志、王学理《唐司马睿墓清理简报》，《考古与文物》1985年第1期	同上
男骑马俑Ⅰ式	2	长30、通高37厘米	1978年10月~1979年1月	同上	段蕳璧墓	唐高宗永徽二年（651年）	昭陵博物馆《唐昭陵段蕳璧墓清理简报》，《文博》1989年第6期	同上

男骑马俑II式	2	长30、通高35.5厘米	同上	同上	同上	同上	同上
胡俑	2	高17厘米	1989年9月	同上	董僧利及其妻王氏墓	唐高宗永徽三年（652年）	西安市文物管理处《唐董僧利墓清理简报》，《考古与文物》1991年4月	被破坏
胡人侍俑	1	高45厘米	2001年秋	山西襄垣	浩宽墓	唐高宗永徽六年（655年）	山西大学文博学院、襄垣县文物博物馆《山西襄垣唐代浩氏家族墓》，《文物》2004年第10期	该墓编号为2001M32；积水和墓顶塌落土，随葬品已被扰乱
胡人牵马俑	1	同上	同上	同上	同上	同上	同上	同上
胡人俑	1	高20厘米	2000年9月	河南洛阳	宗光墓	同上	洛阳市文物工作队 司马国红《河南洛阳市东郊十里铺村唐墓》，《考古》2007年第9期	该墓编号为C5M1532；被盗
胡俑I式	4	高29.5厘米	1983年5月	河南安阳	廍伎墓	唐高宗显庆元年（656年）	安阳市博物馆《安阳市第二制药厂唐墓发掘简报》，《中原文物》1986年第3期	该墓编号为M1
胡俑II式	2	同上	同上	同上	同上	同上	同上	同上
男胡立俑	4（I式2件，II式2件）	I式高26厘米，II式高23.5厘米	1972年1月	陕西礼泉	张士贵墓	唐高宗显庆二年（657年）	陕西省文管会、昭陵文管所《陕西礼泉唐张士贵墓》，《考古》1978年第3期	被盗
男胡牵马俑	2	高38厘米	同上	同上	同上	同上	同上	同上
男骑马胡俑	6	同上	同上	同上	同上	同上	同上	同上
骑站驼胡俑	1	残高26厘米	1960年7月	山西长治	乐方墓	唐高宗显庆四年（659年）	山西省文物管理委员会晋南文物工作组《山西长治北石槽唐墓》，《考古》1965年第9期	该墓编号为六号墓；因墓顶已塌陷，故绝大部分被砸毁，此墓为迁葬、合葬墓
胡俑	1	高29.5厘米	1986年7月	同上	范澄夫妇墓	唐高宗显庆五年（660年）	长治市博物馆《长治县宋家庄唐代范澄夫妇墓》，《文物》1989年第6期	
御驼俑	1	高27厘米	同上	同上	同上	同上	同上	
骑马俑	1	残高31厘米	1980年秋	陕西西安	张楚贤墓	唐高宗龙朔二年（662年）	桑绍华《西安南郊三爻村发现四座唐墓》，《考古与文物》1983年第3期	该墓编号为M1；该墓遭破坏
胡人俑	2	高26厘米	1988年4月	河南偃师	柳凯夫妇墓	唐高宗麟德元年（664年）	洛阳市第二文物工作队、偃师县文物管理委员会《河南偃师唐柳凯墓》，《文物》1992年第12期	该墓编号为M19；随葬品绝大多数保持原来位置
胡帽俑I式	8	高28.5厘米	同上	同上	同上	同上	同上	同上
胡帽俑II式	1	高26厘米	同上	同上	同上	同上	同上	同上
男立俑III式	21	高29厘米	1972年	陕西礼泉	郑仁泰墓	同上	陕西省博物馆、礼泉县文教局《唐郑仁泰墓发掘简报》，《文物》1972年第7期	被盗和遭破坏
卷发俑	1	高30厘米	同上	同上	同上	同上	同上	同上
男骑俑	42	通高40厘米	同上	同上	同上	同上	同上	同上
男骑俑			同上	同上	同上	同上	《中国美术全集·雕塑编》第4册《隋唐雕塑》，人民美术出版社1988年	
幞头骑马侍从俑I型	1	残高42、通长45厘米	1984年4月	陕西西安	赵行□夫妻合葬墓	唐高宗麟德□年	关双喜、师晓群《西安东郊出土的一批汉唐文物》，《文博》1985年第6期	
昆仑俑	1	高27厘米	1985年5月	陕西长武	张臣合墓	唐高宗总章元年（668年）	长武县博物馆《陕西长武郭村唐墓》，《文物》2004年第2期	被盗，墓室进水积满淤泥，随葬品已被扰乱
胡俑	1	高25厘米	同上	同上	同上	同上	同上	同上
胡人俑	1	高30.5厘米	1987年春	河北清河	孙建墓	唐高宗咸亨元年（670年）	辛明伟、李振奇《河北清河丘家那唐墓》，《文物》1990年第7期	该墓编号为M1；大部分保存完好，位置清楚
胡人俑（戴方顶护颈风帽）	2	座长8、宽7、通高26.5厘米	1977年5月	河北文安	董满墓	唐高宗咸亨三年（672年）	廊坊市文物管理所、文安县文物管理所《河北文安麻各庄唐墓》，《文物》1994年第1期	随葬品乃收集得到的
胡人俑（戴尖顶风帽）	1	座长8、宽7、通高29厘米	同上	同上	同上	同上	同上	同上

昆仑奴俑	1	座长7、宽6.5、通高22.5厘米	同上	同上	同上	同上	同上
胡俑	1		1965年5月	辽宁朝阳	左才墓	唐高宗咸亨四年（673年）	辽宁省博物馆文物队《辽宁朝阳唐左才墓》，《文物资料丛刊》第6期，1982年	该墓大部分保存完好
马年、驼年俑Ⅰ式	2	高24.5厘米	1975年10月	河南安阳	杨偘及其妻李氏合葬墓	杨偘唐高宗永徽五年（654年）李氏唐高宗上元二年（675年）	安阳市博物馆《唐杨偘墓清理简报》，《文物数据丛刊》第6期，1982年	地下水的破坏
吐蕃俑	5		同上	同上	同上	同上	同上	同上
胡人牵马（驼）俑	3	高25.5、底长5.6厘米	1993年12月	山西长治	王惠墓	唐高宗上元三年（676年）	长治市博物馆《山西长治唐代王惠墓》，《文物》2003年第8期	该墓编号为M1；墓室内随葬品基本保持原有位置
胡人骑驼俑	1	高76.5、长68厘米	同上	同上	同上	同上	同上
胡人骑马俑	3	高44、长45.2厘米	同上	同上	同上	同上	同上
单髻俑	1	高18.1厘米	2000年3月	河南郑州	丁彻及其妻韩氏合葬墓	同上	郑州市文物考古研究所《郑州唐丁彻墓发掘简报》，《华夏考古》2000年第4期	该墓编号为2000ZKCM1
男胡俑	1	残高4.6厘米	1982年11月	宁夏固原	史道德墓	唐高宗仪凤三年（678年）	宁夏固原博物馆《宁夏固原唐史道德墓清理简报》，《文物》1985年第11期	被盗
骑骆驼胡俑	1		1954年4月	山西长治	王深墓	唐高宗调露元年（679年）	山西省文物管理委员会《山西长治唐墓清理简报》，《考古通讯》1957年第5期	该墓保存状况比较好，随葬品大部分都保持原状
骑驼老年胡俑	1	通高70厘米	1960年7月	同上	乐道仁墓	唐睿宗文明元年（684年）	山西省文物管理委员会晋南文物工作组《山西长治北石槽唐墓》，《考古》1965年第9期	此墓编号为四号墓；虽墓顶塌陷，但随葬器物并未改变位置
牵驼胡俑（牵站驼）	1	高49厘米	同上	同上	同上	同上	同上
牵驼胡俑（牵卧驼）	1	残高54厘米	同上	同上	同上	同上	同上
彩绘骑马男胡俑		高36厘米	1998年	河南偃师	唐恭陵哀皇后墓	武则天垂拱元年（685年）	洛阳市文物管理局编《洛阳陶俑》，北京图书出版社2005年5月	
胡人俑	10	高23厘米	1992年	陕西岐山	元师奖墓	武则天垂拱二年（686年）	宝鸡市考古队《歧山郑家村唐元师奖墓清理简报》，《考古与文物》1994年第3期	多次被盗，致使随葬器物损坏严重，组合关系不清楚
男侍俑	3	高19.5厘米	同上	同上	同上	同上	同上	同上
风帽俑	1	通高42厘米	1986年3月	河北南和	郭祥夫妇合葬墓	武则天垂拱四年（688年）	辛明伟、李振奇《河北南和唐代郭祥墓》，《文物》1993年第6期	随葬陶俑大部分保存完整，且数量多，品类全；部分随葬品的位置被扰乱
胡人俑	2	37号带座通高26厘米，38号带座通高23.2厘米	同上	同上	同上	同上	同上	同上
牵驼俑	1	高40.5厘米	1991年8月	陕西西安	于隐及金乡县主墓	武周永昌元年（689年）～天授元年（690年）	西安市文物保护考古研王自力、孙福喜编著《唐金乡县主墓》，文物出版社2002年	墓室和甬道的随葬品大多被盗，东、西两龛没遭盗劫，随葬品保存尚好
牵马俑Ⅰ型	2	91XYS：114通高43厘米，91XYS：112通高42.5厘米	同上	同上	同上	同上	同上	同上
牵马俑Ⅳ型	1	通高38.7厘米	同上	同上	同上	同上	同上	同上
骑立驼俑	1	通高63、骆驼长56厘米	同上	同上	同上	同上	同上	同上
骑卧驼俑	1	通高41、骆驼长61厘米	同上	同上	同上	同上	同上	同上

抱犬狩猎胡俑	2	91XYX：25通高35.5、马长33.5厘米，91XYD：48通高30.3、马长24厘米	同上	同上	同上	同上	同上	骑马狩猎俑 I 型
架鹰狩猎胡俑	2	91XYX：23通高37.5、马长33.5厘米，91XYX：27通高34.8、马长32.4厘米	同上	同上	同上	同上	同上	骑马狩猎俑 II 型
带豹狩猎胡俑	1	通高35.5、马长34厘米	同上	同上	同上	同上	同上	骑马狩猎俑 III 型
狩猎胡俑	1	通高29.2、马长22厘米	同上	同上	同上	同上	同上	骑马狩猎俑 IV 型
高髻女俑	1	通高26厘米	同上	同上	同上	同上	同上	中型女立俑 III 型
参军戏俑	1	通高6.4厘米	同上	同上	同上	同上	同上	
三彩男牵马俑	2	通高33厘米	1991年秋	河南洛阳	屈突季礼墓	武则天天授二年（691年）	310国道孟津考古队《洛阳孟津西头山唐墓发掘报告》，《华夏考古》1993年第1期	该墓编号为M64；墓葬保存基本完整，随葬品保持原来位置
男牵马俑	1	通高22厘米	同上	同上	同上	同上	同上	同上
陶驭手俑	2	一件高26厘米，另一件高28厘米	1986年10月	山西长治	冯廓夫妇墓	武则天天授二年（691年）	长治市博物馆《山西长治市唐代冯廓墓》，《文物》1989年第6期	墓内随葬品群众被取出，位置不明
陶踞坐俑	1	高19厘米	同上	同上	同上	同上	同上	同上
胡服骑马俑	4	M1：东龛16通高30.8、马长23.4、马高25.6厘米	2000年12月~2001年1月	陕西西安	温思暕墓	武则天万岁登封元年（696年）	西安市文物保护考古所《西安东郊唐温绰、温思暕墓发掘简报》，《文物》2002年第12期	该墓编号为M1；墓室被盗，而壁龛尚未被盗扰；骑马俑的F型
舞俑	2	高31厘米	1958年6月	同上	独孤思贞墓	武则天神功元年（697年）	独孤思贞墓，见于中国社会科学院考古研究所编著《唐长安城郊隋唐墓》，文物出版社1980年9月	仅墓室被扰乱，其它部分保存尚好
骑马乐俑（歌唱状）	2	通高35~38厘米	同上	同上	同上	同上	同上	同上
牵驼俑	4	高52厘米	同上	同上	同上	同上	同上	同上
三彩牵马俑	1	通高44.4、底板厚0.9厘米	2002年6月	同上	康文通墓	同上	西安市文物保护考古所《唐康文通墓发掘简报》，《文物》2004年第1期	该墓编号为M2；被盗
三彩风帽男骑俑	1	长30、高36厘米	1999年6月	同上	姚无陂墓	同上	西安市文物保护考古所《唐姚无陂墓发掘简报》，《文物》2002年第12期	
三彩幞头男俑	2	通高23厘米	同上	同上	同上	同上	同上	
男侍俑	4	高26厘米	2002年7月	山西襄垣	李石夫妇墓	武则天久视元年（700年）	山西大学文博学院、襄垣县文物博物馆《山西襄垣唐代李石夫妇合葬墓》，《文物》2004年第10期	该墓编号为2002M3；随葬陶俑多被破坏，位置被扰乱，散于墓室各处
牵马俑	2	通高61.7厘米	1991年9月	河南洛阳	岑平等墓	武则天大足元年（701年）	310国道孟津考古队《洛阳孟津西山头唐墓》，《文物》1992年第3期	该墓编号为M69；被盗，但俑道随葬品保存良好
牵驼俑	2	通高58厘米	同上	同上	同上	同上	同上	同上
三彩男侍胡俑	2	通高36厘米	1985年秋	河南偃师	张思忠墓	武则天长安三年（703年）	偃师县文物管理委员会《河南偃师县隋唐墓发掘简报》，《考古》1986年第11期	此墓编号为85YYMI；被破坏
胡俑	1	高3.5厘米	1961年4月	山西长治	王义墓	武则天长安四年（704年）	山西省文物管理委员会、山西省考古研究所《山西长治北石槽唐墓》，《考古》1962年第2期	报告中的二号墓；虽墓顶塌陷，随葬品多被砸毁，但原来位置基本未变
骑立驼胡俑	1	通高65厘米	同上	同上	同上	同上	同上	同上
三彩牵马俑			1971年7月~1972年2月	陕西西安	唐章怀太子墓	唐中宗神龙二年（706年）	陕西省博物馆、乾县文教局《唐章怀太子墓发掘简报》，《文物》1972年第7期	被盗

名称	数量	尺寸	出土时间	出土地点	墓葬	年代	著录	备注
男骑胡俑	18	高27.8～31.2厘米	1960年8月～1962年4月	同上	同上	同上	陕西省文物管理委员会《唐永泰公主墓发掘简报》，《文物》1964年第1期	
男骑胡俑		高30.3厘米	同上	同上	同上	同上	《中国美术全集·雕塑编》第4册《隋唐雕塑》，人民美术出版社1988年	
三彩男立胡俑	24	高20厘米	同上	同上	同上	同上	陕西省文物管理委员会《唐永泰公主墓发掘简报》，《文物》1964年第1期	
三彩男骑胡俑	1	残高10.8厘米	同上	同上	同上	同上	同上	
胡俑头像	1	残高14.5厘米	同上	同上	同上	同上	《中国美术全集·雕塑编》第4册《隋唐雕塑》，人民美术出版社1988年	
胡俑头像	1	残高9.7厘米	同上	同上	同上	同上	同上	
男骑马俑	不明	残高30～37厘米	1959年1月	陕西长安	韦泂墓	同上	陕西省文物管理委员会《长安县南里王村唐韦泂墓发掘记》，《文物》1959年第8期	该墓早年被盗，后期前后墓室遭严重破坏
胡服俑	5	通高24～26厘米	1957年2月	河南偃师	崔沈墓	同上	河南省文化局文物工作队《河南偃师唐崔沈墓发掘简报》，《文物参考数据》1958年第8期	随葬品保持着原来的位置
陶牵马俑	3（灰陶者2件，红陶者1件）	灰陶者高51、宽17.5厘米，红陶者高高6.5、宽3.8厘米	1954年7月	陕西西安	任氏墓	唐中宗神龙三年（707年）	陕西省文物管理委员会《西安郭家汉唐墓清理简报》，《考古通讯》1956年第6期	该墓编号为第395号；积水和淤泥的关系，随葬品位置已移动
辫发男俑II型	1	通高46.5厘米	1956年	同上	郭恒墓	唐中宗景龙二年（708年）	中国社会科学院考古研究所编著《西安郊区隋唐墓》，科学出版社1966年	该墓编号为墓203；被盗
幞头牵马胡俑I型	4		同上	同上	同上	同上	同上	同上
骑马俑	4	M5：33通高39厘米，M5：27通高39厘米	1984年春	河南偃师	李延祯墓	唐中宗景龙三年（709年）	中国社会科学院考古研究所河南第二工作队《河南偃师杏园村的两座唐墓》，《考古》1984年第10期	此墓编号为84YDT19M5；没被盗，形制保存完好
牵马俑	2	M5：43通高33厘米	同上	同上	同上	同上	同上	同上
牵驼俑	2	M5：64通高35.5厘米	同上	同上	同上	同上	同上	同上
御者	1		同上	同上	同上	同上	同上	同上
男侍胡俑	不明	23厘米	同上	同上	同上	同上	同上	同上
骑马男侍俑	1	通高38.8厘米	1984年夏季至1985年秋季	同上	李嗣本墓	同上	中国社会科学院考古研究所河南第二工作队《河南偃师杏园村的六座纪年唐墓》，《考古》1986年第5期	该墓编号为84YDM1928
男骑马俑	4	通高38厘米	同上	同上	同上	同上	中国社会科学院考古研究所编著《偃师杏园唐墓》，科学出版社2001年	同上
牵马俑	1	通高50厘米	同上	同上	同上	同上	同上	该墓编号为84YDM1928；牵夫俑A型
牵驼胡俑	1	通高49厘米	同上	同上	同上	同上	中国社会科学院考古研究所河南第二工作队《河南偃师杏园村的六座纪年唐墓》，《考古》1986年第5期	该墓编号为84YDM1928；牵夫俑B型
牵驼俑	1	通高52.5厘米	同上	同上	同上	同上	中国社会科学院考古研究所编著《偃师杏园唐墓》，科学出版社2001年	该墓编号为84YDM1928；牵夫俑B型
御扶者	1	通高23.1厘米	同上	同上	同上	同上	中国社会科学院考古研究所河南第二工作队《河南偃师杏园村的六座纪年唐墓》，《考古》1986年第5期	该墓编号为84YDM1928
男侍俑	3	通高31.7厘米	同上	同上	同上	同上	中国社会科学院考古研究所编著《偃师杏园唐墓》，科学出版社2001年	该墓编号为84YDM1928；男侍俑B型
文吏俑	2	俑1高75.5厘米，俑2高74.3厘米	1956年12月	陕西西安	独孤思敬及其妻元氏合葬墓	同上	中国社会科学院考古研究所编著《唐长安城郊隋唐墓》，文物出版社1980年	被盗，墓室等均遭扰乱
牵马俑	4	俑9高51.3厘米，俑10高52.9厘米，俑11高52.9厘米，俑14高51厘米	同上	同上	同上	同上	同上	同上

牵驼俑	4	俑8高79.4厘米，俑12高82.4厘米，俑13高80.9厘米	同上	同上	同上	同上	同上	同上
骑驼男俑	1	俑7高41.6厘米	同上	同上	同上	同上		同上
三彩牵马牵驼俑I式	2	M27：63高59厘米，M27：64高67厘米	1981年4月下旬	河南洛阳	安菩及其妻何氏合葬墓	同上	洛阳市文物工作队《洛阳龙门唐安菩夫妇墓》，《中原文物》1982年第3期	该墓编号为C7M27
三彩牵马牵驼俑II式	2	通高62厘米	同上	同上	同上	同上	同上	同上
三彩男骑马乐俑II式	2	通高43、长39厘米	同上	同上	同上	同上	同上	同上
三彩牵马牵驼俑	不明	通高73～82厘米	1965年9月～1966年初	甘肃秦安		景龙三年（或神龙三年）	甘肃省博物馆文物队《甘肃秦安县唐墓清理简报》，《文物》1975年第4期	该墓被编号为一号墓；被盗
三彩男骑马俑	1		同上	同上	同上	同上	同上	同上
文官俑	1	高94.5厘米	1995年	陕西富平	节愍太子墓	唐睿宗景云元年（710年）	陕西省考古研究所、富平县文物管理委员会编著《唐节愍太子墓发掘报告》，科学出版社2004年	被盗
武官俑	1	高100厘米	同上	同上	同上	同上	同上	同上
牵骆驼男俑	2	高63.5厘米	1991年12月	河南孟县	程最墓	唐玄宗开元五年（717年）	焦作市文物工作队、孟县博物馆《河南孟县堤北头唐代程最墓发掘简报》，《中原文物》1995年第4期	被盗
三彩牵马牵驼俑	1	高51厘米	1972年11月	陕西西安	李贞墓	唐玄宗开元六年（718年）	昭陵文物管理所《唐越王李贞发掘简报》，《文物》1977年第10期	被盗、移动、扰乱情况严重
三彩男侍胡俑	1	高42.7厘米	1956年12月～1957年2月	同上	鲜于庭诲墓	唐玄宗开元十一年（723年）	马得志、张正龄《西安郊区三个唐墓的发掘简报》，《考古通讯》1958年第1期	该墓编号为西郊1号墓
三彩牵驼牵马俑	4	俑3高45.2厘米，俑6高45.3厘米，俑1高42.5厘米，俑2高39.8厘米	1957年2月	同上	同上	同上	中国社会科学院考古研究所编著《唐长安城郊隋唐墓》，文物出版社1980年	
三彩卧驼骑俑	1	驼高37.7、通骑俑高39.4、长47厘米	同上	同上	同上	同上	同上	同上
三彩骆驼载乐俑	1	驼高58.4、长43.4厘米，舞俑高25.1厘米	同上	同上	同上	同上	同上	同上
幞头男立俑	3	95HZM：37高30厘米，95HZM：46高30.2厘米，95HZM：61高30.6厘米	1995年10月～1996年5月	陕西蒲城	惠庄太子墓	唐玄宗开元十二年（724年）	陕西省考古研究所《唐惠庄太子李撝墓发掘报告》，科学出版社2004年4月	被盗；男立俑Cb型
风帽俑	14	高19.6厘米	2005年	河南洛阳	卢照已墓	同上	洛阳市第二文物工作队《洛阳唐卢照已墓发掘简报》，《文物》2007年第6期	该墓编号为2005LNCM9；被盗
袒胸胡人俑	1	通高50厘米	2001年4月	甘肃庆城	穆泰墓	唐玄宗开元十八年（730年）	庆阳市博物馆、庆城县博物馆《甘肃庆城唐代游击将军穆泰墓》，《文物》2008年第3期	该墓编号为2001M2；被盗
牵犬俑	3	M2：24通高53厘米，M2：25通高50厘米，M2：27通高53厘米	同上	同上	同上	同上	同上	同上
牵驼俑	1	高31.7厘米	2002年4月	陕西西安	孙承嗣及妻高氏合葬墓	唐玄宗开元二十四年（736年）	陕西省考古研究所、西安市文物保护考古所《唐孙承嗣夫妇墓发掘简报》，《考古与文物》2005年第2期	该墓编号为M12；该墓结构完整，出土遗物丰富，纪年明确
胡人俑	2	高18厘米	同上	同上	同上	同上	同上	同上
吹笛俑	1	通高15.7厘米	同上	同上	同上	同上	同上	同上

击钱俑	1	同上	同上	同上	同上	同上	同上
吹筚篥俑	1	通高15.9厘米	同上	同上	同上	同上	似为男装女伎乐俑；柳眉长眼，高鼻小口
吹笙俑	1	同上	同上	同上	同上	同上	该墓编号为M12；该墓结构完整，出土遗物丰富，纪年明确
百戏俑	1	残高12.6厘米	同上	同上	同上	同上	同上
骑马俑	1	通高43.5厘米	1983年7月	同上	俾失十囊墓	唐玄宗开元二十七年（739年）	李域铮《西安西郊唐俾失十囊墓清理简报》，《文博》1985年第6期，	随葬品被群众取出
乐俑	1	通高约8厘米	同上	同上	同上	同上	同上	同上
文官俑	1	残高67厘米	1958年7月	同上	杨思勖墓	唐玄宗开元二十八年（740年）	杨思勖墓，中国社会科学院考古研究所编《唐长安城郊隋唐墓》，文物出版社1980年	被盗
男胡俑	1		同上	同上	同上	同上	同上	同上
陶武臣俑	1	通高70、座高12厘米	1992年9月	河南洛阳	唐睿宗贵妃豆卢氏墓		洛阳市文物工作队《唐睿宗贵妃豆卢氏墓发掘简报》，《文物》1995年第8期	多次被盗
胡人俑	34	通高54厘米	2000年3月~2001年1月	陕西蒲城	李宪墓	唐玄宗开元二十九年（741年）	陕西省考古研究所编《唐李宪墓发掘报告》，科学出版社2005年	墓室被盗，但壁龛保存完好
骑卧驼俑	3	K4：95通高56.4、驼高40.8、长75.2厘米，K5：24通高58.5、驼高45、长78.5厘米，K6：4通高55、驼高48.5、长82.5厘米	同上	同上	同上	同上	同上	同上
牵马牵驼俑I式	5	通高21厘米	1983年2月	河南偃师	李元璹及其妻郑氏合葬墓	同上	洛阳行署文物处、偃师县文管会《偃师唐李元璹夫妇墓发掘简报》，《中原文物》1985年第1期	被盗
胡人风帽骑马俑I型	1	通高31.2、马高27、马长27厘米	2002年10月	陕西西安	韦慎名墓	二次葬（开元十五年，开元二十年）	陕西省考古研究所、西安市文物保护研究所《唐长安南郊韦慎名墓清理简报》，《考古与文物》2003年第6期	该墓出土物保存基本完好
胡人风帽骑马俑II型	7	M101：21通高32.7、马高27、长25.8厘米	同上	同上	同上	同上	同上	同上
蹼头俑II型	2	M101：258通高13.3厘米	同上	同上	同上	同上	同上	同上
胡女俑	1	高28.5厘米	1977年6月	江苏吴县	张子文夫妇合葬墓	唐玄宗天宝二年（743年）	江苏省吴县文管会《江苏吴县姚桥头唐墓》，《文物》1987年第8期	被盗
牵马胡人俑	1	高32厘米	同上	同上	同上	同上	同上	同上
牵马俑			1953年3月	陕西西安	雷府君夫人宋氏墓	唐玄宗天宝四年（745年）	张正岭《西安韩森寨唐墓清理记》，《考古》1957年第5期	该墓未发掘完毕
胡俑头	1		1987年12月	陕西泾阳	张仲晖墓	唐玄宗天宝十二年（753年）	陕西省考古研究所、泾阳县文管会《唐张仲晖墓发掘简报》，《考古与文物》1992年第1期	该墓被严重破坏
蹼头男俑	1	通高32厘米	1985年4月	陕西西安	装利物及其妻窦氏合葬墓	唐肃宗乾元二年（759年）	《西安三桥车辆厂工地发现唐裴利物夫妇墓》，《考古与文物》1991年第6期	该墓塌陷严重
胡人骑俑	2	完整者高37厘米，残缺者残高22厘米	1989年7月	同上	唐安公主墓	唐德宗兴元元年（784年）	陈安利、马咏钟《西安王家坟唐代唐安公主墓》，《文物》1991年第9期	被盗；一件完整，另一件残缺
残胡服男俑	2		1986年9月	陕西西安	唐西昌令夫人史氏墓	唐德宗贞元十一年（795年）	陈安利、马骥《西安西郊唐西昌县令夫人史氏墓》，《考古与文物》1988年第3期	该墓破坏严重
男立俑	14	通高31厘米	1948年	陕西长安	裴氏小娘子墓	唐宣宗大中四年（850年）	李秀兰、卢桂兰《唐裴氏小娘子墓出土文物》，《文博》1993年第1期	

牵马胡人俑 Ⅰ式	2	高30厘米	同上	同上	同上	同上	同上	
牵马胡人俑 Ⅱ式	4	同上	同上	同上	同上	同上	同上	
黑人俑Ⅰ	1	高15厘米	同上	同上	同上	同上	同上	
黑人俑Ⅱ	1	高14.7厘米	同上	同上	同上	同上	同上	
黑人俑	2	裸者高14.5厘米，穿袍者高14.3厘米	同上	同上	同上	同上	《中国美术全集·雕塑编》第4册《隋唐雕塑》，人民美术出版社1988年	
胡人半身俑	2	高12、宽7、厚6厘米			陕西永寿			
胡人俑	3	残高37厘米	1956年4月		湖北武汉	上限在开皇元年，下限在武德四年	湖北省文物管理委员会《武汉市郊周家湾241号墓隋墓清理简报》，《考古通讯》1957年第6期	该墓编号为241号墓；此墓破坏严重，随葬品位置已乱，多发现于四个耳室内
胡俑Ⅱ型	2	M105：1高15厘米	1990年12月		陕西西安	唐代	西安市文物管理处《西安西郊热电厂基建工地隋唐墓葬清理简报》，《考古与文物》1991年第4期	该墓破坏严重
牵马牵驼俑	4	高51.5厘米	1979年6月		甘肃宁县	同上	许俊臣《甘肃宁县出土唐代彩绘俑》，《考古与文物》1982年第4期	被盗
胡立俑	2	残高22厘米	1976年		宁夏银川	同上	宁夏回族自治区博物馆《银川附近的汉墓和唐墓》，《文物》1978年第8期	该墓的编号为一号墓；破坏严重
牵驼胡俑	1	高34、宽13厘米	同上		同上		同上	该墓的编号为八号墓；破坏严重
女胡头俑	2	一件高9厘米，另一件高5.5厘米	同上		同上		同上	同上
胡俑头	1	头径11×6厘米	同上		同上		同上	该墓的编号为六号墓
男侍俑	5	高30厘米	1971年9月		湖南湘阴	同上	湖南省博物馆《湖南湘阴唐墓清理简报》，《文物》1972年第11期	被盗
胡俑	1	高33厘米	1957年		天津	同上	天津市文化局考古发掘队《天津军粮城发现的唐代墓葬》，《考古》1963年第3期	此墓早年曾受破坏，故墓室结构不详
男立俑Ⅰ式	2	M87：20高30.8厘米	1983年～1984年		陕西凤翔	同上	雍城考古队《陕西凤翔县城南郊唐墓群发掘简报》，《考古与文物》1989年第5期	该墓编号为M87
半身俑	1		1987年		陕西陇县	同上	王桂枝、胡百川《陕西陇县东南乡党家庄唐墓发掘简报》，《考古与文物》1990年第1期	被盗
牵马俑	2	93HGSM1：9高33厘米	1993年11月		河南巩义	同上	郑州市文物考古研究所、巩义市文物保护管理所《巩义市食品厂唐墓发掘简报》，《中原文物》2003年第4期	该墓编号为93HGSM1
牵马俑	2	93HGSM2：4高23厘米	同上		同上	同上	同上	该墓编号为93HGSM2
牵驼胡俑	1	高35.2厘米			陕西礼泉		同上	《中国美术全集·雕塑编》第4册《隋唐雕塑》，人民美术出版社1988年	陕西省博物馆藏
骑马胡俑	1				同上		同上	同上	同上
骑马胡俑	1				同上		同上	同上	同上
黑人杂技俑	1	高27.7厘米			传陕西西安		同上	同上	中国历史博物馆藏
大食行旅俑	1	高29.3厘米			同上		同上	同上	同上
大食人立俑	1	高26.3厘米			同上		同上	同上	同上
彩绘男胡俑		高23厘米	1986年		河南洛阳		同上	洛阳市文物管理局编《洛阳陶俑》，北京图书出版社，2005年	
彩绘男胡俑		高39厘米	1980年		河南偃师		同上		

褐釉牵马男胡俑		高36厘米	1985年	同上		同上	同上
三彩牵马男胡俑		高46厘米	1971年	河南洛阳		同上	同上
三彩牵马男胡俑		高66厘米	1963年	同上		同上	同上
三彩牵驼男胡俑		高31.2厘米	1974年	河南偃师		同上	同上
胡人俑1式	4	M4∶16高34厘米	1994年4月	湖南岳阳	唐代早期	岳阳市文物考古研究所《湖南岳阳桃花山唐墓》，《文物》2006年第11期	该墓编号为M4；被盗
胡人俑2式	2	M4∶19高34厘米另一件高27厘米	同上	同上	同上	同上	同上
胡人俑3式	1	高27厘米	同上	同上	同上	同上	同上
男侍俑Ⅲ式	1	通高17厘米	2000年11月	河南三门峡	唐代早期	三门峡市文物考古研究所《三门峡三里桥村11号唐墓》，《中原文物》2003年第3期	该墓编号为M11
胡俑	数件		1977年5月	江苏扬州	同上	李万、张亚《扬州出土一批唐代彩绘俑》，《文物》1979年第4期	该墓破坏严重
陶男侍俑Ⅰ型	1	通高20.2厘米	2005年7月	河南洛阳	唐代中期	洛阳市第二文物工作队《洛阳关林大道徐屯东段唐墓发掘简报》，《文物》2006年第11期	该墓编号为LNGM38；被盗；随葬品保存状况较好
陶男侍俑Ⅱ型	1	通高20.2厘米	同上	同上	同上	同上	同上
陶男侍俑Ⅲ型	1	通高20厘米	同上	同上	同上	同上	同上
陶男侍俑Ⅳ型	2	LNGM38∶20高20.2厘米LNGM38∶21高19.8厘米	同上	同上	同上	同上	同上
男胡俑	1	高25厘米	1972年3月	江苏扬州	同上	扬州市博物馆《扬州发现两座唐墓》，《文物》1973年第5期	该墓遭到严重破坏
胡俑	2	无残者（1∶8）高23厘米	1980年	河北献县	同上	王敏之、高良谟、张长虹《河北献县唐墓清理简报》，《文物》1990年第5期	其中1件上身已残缺；该墓编号为XM1；位置被扰乱；墓主人可能为中下级官吏；圆形墓
彩绘男胡俑		高23.5厘米	2001年	河南偃师	初唐时期	洛阳市文物管理局编《洛阳陶俑》，北京图书出版社，2005年5月	
骑马男俑	1	高17.2厘米	1986年	河南洛阳	同上	洛阳市文物工作队《洛阳孟津朝阳送庄唐墓简报》，《中原文物》2007年第6期	该墓编号为C10M821；被盗；细目高鼻
蹼头男骑俑	2		1981年1月	陕西西安	同上	张海云、廖彩梁、张铭惠《西安市西郊曹家堡唐墓清理简报》，《考古与文物》1986年第2期	着胡服
胡俑	1	通高21.8厘米	1988年10月	陕西宝鸡	同上	宝鸡市考古队《千阳坡头唐墓清理简报》，《考古与文物》1995年第3期	该墓编号为M1；没有提及组合关系
武吏俑	10	高22～27厘米	1978年8月	四川万县	冉仁才墓	初唐时期（永徽五年年）	四川省博物馆《四川万县唐墓》，《考古学报》1980年第4期	墓室和墓室耳室被盗
青瓷文吏俑	数件		同上	同上	同上	同上	同上
青瓷男侍立俑	5		同上	同上	同上	同上	穿胡服
青瓷牵马牵驼俑	3		同上	同上	同上	同上	
牵骆驼俑	2	通高26厘米	1959年	河南洛阳	初唐时期	洛阳市博物馆《洛阳清理一座唐墓》，《文物》1965年第7期	该墓的编号为M2；因墓道进水，器物被冲乱
男胡侍俑	1	高26厘米	1975年5月	湖南长沙		湖南省博物馆《湖南长沙咸嘉湖唐墓发掘简报》，《考古》1980年第6期	被盗
男侍俑	3	分别高27、28、30厘米	1956年7月	同上		湖南省文物管理委员会《长沙黄土岭唐墓清理记》，《考古通讯》1958年第3期	该墓编号为56长黄M024号；被盗和遭破坏；穿胡服

胡俑	2	高29～31厘米，方座宽6－9、厚2厘米	1963年7月	同上	同上		何介钧、交道义《湖南长沙牛角塘唐墓》，《考古》1964年第12期	此墓编号为63长牛M1；其随葬品大多分布在墓室的两端、棺床的外面
胡人俑	1	通高约11厘米	1986年9月	河南西平	同上		驻马店地区文化局、西平县文化局《西平唐墓发掘简报》，《中原文物》1988年第1期	被盗
胡人俑	1	残高18厘米	1972年5月	江苏无锡	同上		无锡市博物馆《江苏无锡发现唐墓》，《文物资料丛刊》第6期，1982年	陶典村墓
风帽俑	2	高22厘米	2003年10月	河南洛阳	初唐晚段或晚唐早段		洛阳市文物工作《河南洛阳市关林1305号唐墓的清理》，《考古》2006年第2期	该墓编号为C7M1305；被盗，随葬品的位置和组合情况已不清楚；特征为高鼻
胡俑	2	M1305：55 高29.5厘米，M1305：44 高27.5厘米	同上	同上	同上		同上	同上
胡服俑	1	高30.5厘米	1972年4月	河北定县	唐代早期		信立祥《定县南关唐墓发掘简报》，《文物数据丛刊》第6期，1982年	
三彩牵马俑	2	高29厘米	2001年1月	河南巩义	唐高宗上元至调露年间		郑州市文物考古研究所、巩义市文物保护管理所《河南巩义市老城砖厂唐墓发掘简报》，《华夏考古》2006年第1期	该墓编号为01ZGLCM2；被盗
男骑马俑Ⅰ型	3	89电材：39通高31.4厘米	1989年7月	陕西西安	唐高宗时期前后		张全民、王自力《西安东郊清理的两座唐墓》，《考古与文物》1992年第5期	该墓编号为89电材；深目宽鼻
男骑马俑Ⅱ型	1	89电材：35通高21.7厘米	同上	同上	同上		同上	同上
胡俑	1	通高23.5厘米	1990年春	河南偃师	唐高宗时期前后		偃师商城博物馆《偃师县沟口头砖厂唐墓发掘简报》，《考古与文物》1999年第5期	该墓编号为90YNGM1；保存尚好
胡俑	1	通高36.3厘米	1992年12月初	河南巩义	咸亨三年（642年）至神龙二年（706年）前后		郑州市文物考古研究所、巩义市文物保护管理所《河南省巩义市孝西村唐墓发掘简报》，《文物》1998年第11期	该墓编号为GS92M01；被盗，墓室破坏较严重
文吏俑	2	M35：31通高55.5厘米	同上	同上	咸亨三年（642年）至长寿三年（694年）前后		同上	该墓编号为92HGZM35；被盗；深目高鼻
胡俑	2	M35：21通高18.7厘米	同上	同上	同上		同上	同上
御手俑	2	M36：19通高18.7厘米	同上	同上	同上		同上	该墓编号为92HGZM36
牵马俑	1	通高30厘米	1985年初	陕西西安	睿宗到玄宗初期		马咏钟《西安狄寨出土唐三彩》，《文博》1994年第1期	该墓被破坏已尽
男立俑Ⅳ式	1	高26.5厘米	1983年～1984年	陕西凤翔	武则天至中宗时期		雍城考古队《陕西凤翔县城南郊唐墓群发掘简报》，《考古与文物》1989年第5期	出自M17
三彩男侍俑	5	通高19.8、板厚1厘米	1978年4月	同上	武周初年		赵丛苍《凤翔出土一批唐三彩和陶俑》，《文博》1989年第3期	出土于太相寺唐墓
胡人俑	3	通高25厘米	1992年	河南巩义	武则天时期		河南省文物考古研究所、巩义市文物保管所《巩义市北窑湾汉晋唐五代墓葬》，《考古学报》1996年第3期	该墓编号为92GZBM6；被盗
风帽俑	1	带座通高50厘米	1990年5月	河北南和	武则天垂拱前后		李振奇、辛明伟《河北南和东贾郭唐墓》，《文物》1993年第6期	墓室已遭严重破坏；随葬品除确知武士俑置于甬道两侧龛内，其余仅知置于棺台前，排列顺序已不明
胡人俑	1	带座通高29厘米	同上	同上	同上		同上	同上

名称	数量	尺寸	出土时间	出土地点		年代	著录	备注
三彩胡俑	4	通高29厘米	1991年	河南偃师		武则天长安三年（703年）前后	偃师商城博物馆《河南偃师县四座唐墓发掘简报》，《考古》1992年第11期	此墓编号为91YBCM5，北窑村五号墓；位置较零散
牵马俑	3	M6：23高23厘米 M6：18高30厘米	1972年3月	河南洛阳		武则天晚期或稍后	洛阳市文物工作队《河南洛阳涧西谷水唐墓清理简报》，《考古》1983年第5期	此墓编号为M6；被盗
绿釉男侍从俑	1	高28厘米	同上	同上		同上	同上	同上
陶男侍胡俑	2	M1：2高34.4、肩宽10.8厘米，M1：5高22.5、肩宽6.4厘米	1985年1月	陕西宝鸡		武则天光宅元年（684年）至玄宗开元年间的盛唐时期	宝鸡市考古工作队《宝鸡市谭家村春秋及唐代墓》，《考古》1991年第5期	因系施工队取出，各件原摆放位置均不清
陶骑驼胡俑	1	高44.5厘米	同上	同上		同上	同上	同上
牵马俑	4	高29.4厘米	1988年	河南巩义		700～720年	郑州市文物考古研究所编著《巩义芝田晋唐墓葬》，科学出版社2003年	该墓编号为88HGZM38；随葬品位置基本未变
胡帽俑	1	高36厘米	1992年	同上		690～700年	同上	该墓编号为92HGSM1
牵马俑	2	M34：7通高33厘米，M34：8通高30.7厘米	2002年7月	陕西西安		唐玄宗开元时期	西安市文物保护考古所《西安西北政法学院南校区34号唐墓发掘简报》，《文物》2002年第12期	该墓编号为M34；黑发中分，两侧抓髻
牵驼俑	1	通高33厘米	同上	同上		同上	西安市文物保护考古所《西安西北政法学院南校区34号唐墓发掘简报》，《文物》2002年第12期	
幞头男侍俑V式	1	通高27.8厘米	1990年12月	同上		唐玄宗至唐代宗时期	西安市文物管理处《西安西郊热电厂基建工地隋唐墓葬清理简报》，《考古与文物》1991年第4期	该墓破坏严重
胡俑Ⅰ型	2	M91：29高7.5厘米	同上	同上		同上	同上	同上
牵马（驼）俑	3	第1件高60厘米，第2件高57厘米，第4件高57厘米	1988年1月	同上		同上	西安市文物园林管理局《西安东郊红旗电机厂唐墓》，《文物》1992年第9期	墓室被严重破坏
胡人骑驼俑	1	高57、长60厘米	1988年1月	同上		同上	西安市文物园林管理局《西安东郊红旗电机厂唐墓》，《文物》1992年第9期	墓室被严重破坏
黄釉男胡俑		高30厘米	1972年	河南洛阳		盛唐时期	洛阳市文物管理局编《洛阳陶俑》，北京图书出版社2005年	
黄釉男胡俑		高22.8厘米	同上	同上		同上	同上	
黄釉男胡俑		高24.3厘米	同上	同上		同上	同上	
武士俑A型	1	残高22厘米	1998年5月	河北安国		盛唐前期	河北省考古研究所、保定市文物管理处、安国市文物管理所《河北省安国市梨园唐墓发掘简报》，《文物春秋》2001年第3期	该墓编号为98LYM5；被盗；高鼻大口
文吏俑A型	1	通高40厘米	同上	同上		同上	同上	该墓编号为98LYM4；被盗；浓眉大眼，高鼻大嘴
胡俑A型	1	通高26.7厘米	同上	同上		同上	同上	
胡俑B型	1	通高25厘米	同上	同上		同上	同上	
胡俑C型	2	M4：14通高24.5厘米，M4：12残高19.5厘米	同上	同上		同上	同上	
胡人俑	2	IM2084：15高27.3厘米	2004年6月	河南洛阳		盛唐时期	洛阳市第二文物工作队《洛阳王城大道唐墓（IM2084）发掘简报》，《文物》2005年第8期	该墓编号为IM2084；保存较好
牵驼（马）胡人俑	1	高25.5厘米	同上	同上		同上	同上	同上
三彩武官俑	1	通高49.2、台座高5.6厘米	2002年7月	陕西西安		同上	西安市文物保护考古所《西安南郊唐墓（M31）发掘简报》，《文物》2004年第1期	该墓编号为M31；被盗；深目高鼻

名称	数量	尺寸	时间	出土地点	墓名	年代	出处	备注
三彩牵马俑 I 式	2	通高32厘米	同上	同上		同上	同上	圆脸高鼻，双目突起
三彩牵马俑 II 式	3	通高28厘米	同上	同上		同上	同上	身穿胡服
三彩骑驼奏乐俑	1	通高50.1、长40.5厘米	同上	同上		同上	同上	
三彩胡人俑	1	通高42.6、托板高1厘米	同上	同上		同上	同上	
三彩牵马（驼）俑	3	通高48、踏板厚1.5厘米	1984年12月	同上		同上	陈安利、马咏忠《西安西郊唐墓》，《文物》1990年第7期	
胡俑	1	高5里米	1962年12月	河南上蔡		同上	河南省文化局文物工作队《河南上蔡县贾庄唐墓清理简报》，《文物》1964年第2期	被盗
陶男侍俑	3	高21.5厘米	1988年4月	河南郑州		盛唐时期或稍早	郑州市文物工作队《河南郑州市上街唐墓的清理》，《考古》1996年第8期	该墓编号为SHTM1
胡立俑	2	一件头残，残高25厘米；另一件高29厘米	1980年秋	河南新安		盛唐时期	新安县文管所《河南新安县磁涧出土的唐三彩》，《考古》1987年第9期	
三彩胡俑	1	高45厘米	1984年4月	河南伊川		同上	伊川县大化馆《河南伊川发现一座唐墓》，《考古》1985年第5期	此墓为土洞墓，遭破坏，器物位置已不清楚
拱手男立俑	1	通高29厘米	1956年4月中旬	湖南长沙		同上	湖南省文物管理委员会《湖南长沙唐墓清理记》，《考古通讯》1956年第6期	该墓编号为56长烈园M004；被盗，随葬品均残破不全，位置散乱；此俑穿胡服
骑马武士胡俑	3	通高58厘米	1961年11月底~1962年8月	陕西咸阳	苏君墓	其上限在总章元年以后，下限不会超过开元年间	陕西省社会科学院考古研究所《陕西咸阳唐苏君墓发掘》，《考古》1963年第9期	墓室部分塌陷，曾多次被盗
胡俑	1	高31.5厘米	1959年12月	河南郑州		盛唐（其下限应在玄宗天宝年间）	河南省文化局文物工作队《郑州上街区唐墓发掘简报》，《考古》1960年第1期	该墓编号为墓54
胡俑	1	高35厘米	同上	同上		同上	同上	同上
半身胡俑	1		同上	同上		同上	同上	同上
牵马胡俑	2	高28.5厘米	1959年6月下旬	陕西西安		盛唐时期	陕西省文物管理委员会《西安西郊中堡村唐墓清理简报》，《考古》1960年第3期	墓中部分器物因受淤泥的冲动而失去原来位置
牵驼胡俑	2	高29厘米	同上	同上	同上	同上	同上	同上
三彩骆驼载乐俑	1	通高67厘米	同上	同上		同上	《中国美术全集·雕塑编》第4册《隋唐雕塑》，人民美术出版社1988年	
男骑马俑	2	俑高28、马高52厘米	1981年9月	陕西临潼		盛唐之末（天宝年间）	赵唐民《临潼关山唐墓清理简报》，《考古与文物》1982年第3期	未提及是否被盗
牵马俑	1	高32厘米	同上	同上		同上	同上	同上
牵驼俑	2	高34厘米	同上	同上		同上	同上	同上
说唱俑	1	高7厘米	同上	同上		同上	同上	同上
文吏俑（武官俑）	1	通高72.8、座高12.5~13.5厘米	1996年3月下旬	陕西西安		唐玄宗天宝初年前后	陕西省考古研究所《西安西郊陕棉十厂唐壁画墓清理简报》，《考古与文物》2002年第1期	该墓虽被盗，但出土器物较完整，且大部分位于原摆放的位置；鼻尖高耸
牵马俑	3	M7：61通高32.1厘米	同上	同上		同上	同上	
牵驼俑	1	通高30.8厘米	同上	同上		同上	同上	
胡人俑	1	残高31厘米	1985年春	江苏扬州		中唐时期	扬州博物馆《扬州近年发现唐墓》，《考古》1990年第9期	扬州郭家所唐墓；被盗
三彩牵马人俑	2	通高29厘米	1955年4月	陕西西安		同上	陕西省文物管理委员会《西安东郊十里铺337号唐墓清理简报》，《文物参考数据》1956年第8期	器物的位置大体上没有多大的变化
釉彩牵骆驼人俑	2	通高27.5及28.6厘米	同上	同上		同上	同上	同上

名称	数量	尺寸	时间	地点		时期	出处	备注
男立俑	1		1956年2月	湖北武昌		同上	湖北省文物管理委员会《武昌东郊何家垄188号唐墓清理简报》，《文物参考数据》1957年第12期	该墓保存尚好
男坐俑	1		同上	同上		同上	同上	同上
陶牵马俑	1	高30厘米	2005年7月	河南洛阳		中唐晚段	洛阳市第二文物工作队《洛阳关林大道徐屯东段唐墓发掘简报》，《文物》2006年第11期	该墓编号为LNGM29；被盗；高鼻；墓葬形制清楚，两墓尚能看出放置的次序和规律
风帽俑	4	通高44厘米	1993年7月	辽宁朝阳		8世纪中叶	辽宁省文物考古研究所、朝阳市博物馆《辽宁朝阳市黄河路唐墓的清理》，《考古》2001年第8期	该墓编号为M1；被盗
骑骆驼男俑	1	长59.5、宽28、高73.5厘米	同上	同上		同上	同上	同上
泥俑	1		同上	同上		同上	同上	同上
石男俑	1	通高112厘米	同上	同上		同上	同上	同上
石女俑	1	通高102厘米	同上	同上		同上	同上	同上
胡人男侍俑	1	高33厘米	1980年3月	江苏扬州		中晚唐时期	扬州市博物馆《扬州邗江县杨庙唐墓》，《考古》1983年第9期	该墓被严重破坏
老年胡人男侍俑	1	同上	同上	同上		同上	同上	同上
牵马、牵驼胡人俑	2	高32～33厘米	同上	同上		同上	同上	同上
骑马胡人俑	1		同上	同上		同上	同上	该墓被严重破坏；马腿残，已修复
三彩胡人俑			1986年1月	江西永修		唐代	许智范《文物园地撷英》，《南方文物》1987年第2期	
三彩胡人乐伎俑	1	高8厘米		河南巩义			廖永民《黄冶唐三彩窑址出土的陶塑小品》，《文物》2003年第11期	
三彩骑驼人	1	人驼通高6.5厘米					《巩县黄冶"唐三彩"窑陶瓷玩具》，《考古与文物》1985年第2期	
三彩胡人俑						唐代	林树中主编《海外藏中国历代雕塑》（中册），江西美术出版社2006年	（美）西雅图美术馆藏
胡人立俑		高52厘米				同上	同上	（法）吉美国立东方美术馆藏
胡人俑		高24.5厘米				同上	同上	同上
胡人俑		高30厘米				同上	同上	同上
胡人牵马俑						同上	同上	同上
胡人乐俑		高33.6厘米				同上	林树中主编《海外藏中国历代雕塑》（下册），江西美术出版社2006年	（美）旧金山亚洲美术馆藏
马夫俑						同上	同上	（德）柏林民俗博物馆藏
胡人骑驼俑						同上	同上	（美）托雷多艺术馆藏

（郭桂豪、张鑫收集整理）

责任编辑：李　红　王　伟

装帧设计：李　红

责任印制：陆　联

图书在版编目（CIP）数据

丝路胡人外来风·唐代胡俑展/乾陵博物馆编．－北京：文物
出版社，2008.7

ISBN 978－7－5010－2501－5

Ⅰ．丝… Ⅱ．乾… Ⅲ．①俑－中国－北朝时代（439～
581）－图集②俑－中国－隋唐时代－图集Ⅳ．K878.92

中国版本图书馆CIP数据核字（2008）第079918号

丝路胡人外来风——唐代胡俑展

编　　者：乾陵博物馆

出版发行：文物出版社

地　　址：北京东直门内北小街2号楼

邮　　编：100007

网　　址：http://www.wenwu.com

邮　　箱：web@wenwu.com

经　　销：新华书店

制版印刷：北京画中画印刷有限公司

开　　本：889×1194毫米　1/16

印　　张：13

版　　次：2008年7月第1版

印　　次：2008年7月第1次印刷

书　　号：ISBN 978－7－5010－2501－5

定　　价：190.00元